"In this book, King challenges us to reconsider h
ing'. Focussing on the concept of dwelling, he a
search community shift away from studying the exceptions of policy failure,
to thinking about subjective and individual experiences of housing more
broadly."

– *Dr Helen Taylor, Cardiff Met, UK*

Speculations on the Question: What Is Housing?

This book consists of a single essay that speculates on the question *what is housing?*, and its opposite question, *what is not housing?* The essay is organised around two distinct discourses around which housing can be framed. The first, which is the dominant discourse, is what I term *policy thinking.* This is where housing is seen solely in terms of policy formulation and action. The second discourse is *private dwelling*, which describes housing in terms of a private space used by households. Private dwelling might be seen as a product of policy, but, in actuality, it precedes policy thinking in being the very purpose of policy. Having made this distinction between policy thinking and private dwelling, and so stated in principle what housing is, the subsequent sections of the essay explore the nature of private dwelling in more detail and so substantiate the distinction between the two forms of discourse.

Before retiring in 2018, **Peter King** worked at De Montfort University for 25 years teaching and researching on housing and public policy. He is the author of 22 books including *Thinking on Housing* (2017), *The Principles of Housing* (2015), *In Dwelling* (2008), *The Common Place* (2005) and *Private Dwelling* (2004), all published by Routledge.

Routledge Focus on Housing and Philosophy

Routledge Focus offers both established and early-career academics the flexibility to publish cutting-edge commentary on topical issues, policy-focused research, analytical or theoretical innovations, in-depth case studies or short topics for specialised audiences. The format and speed to market is distinctive. Routledge Focus are 20,000 to 50,000 words and will be published as eBooks, and in Hardback as print on demand.

This book series seeks to develop the links between housing and philosophy. It seeks proposals from academics and policymakers on any aspect of philosophy and its relation to housing. This might include ethics, political and social philosophy, aesthetics as well as logic, epistemology and metaphysics. All proposals would be expected to apply philosophical rigour to the exploration of housing phenomena, whether this be the policymaking process, design or the manner in which individuals and communities relate to housing. The series seeks an international and comparative focus and is particularly keen to include innovative and distinctly new approaches to the study of housing.

Please contact Peter King (*peterking1960@virginmedia.com*) with ideas for a book proposal or for further details.

Books in the series:

Peter King, *Thinking on Housing: Words, Memories, Use*
Helen Taylor, *Social Justice in Contemporary Housing: Applying Rawls'
    Difference Principle*
Joanna Richardson, *Place and Identity: Home as Performance*
Yoric Irving-Clarke, *Supported Housing: Past, Present and Future*
Peter King, *Speculations on the Question: What Is Housing?*

For more information about this series, please visit: https://www.routledge.com

Speculations on the Question: What Is Housing?

Peter King

R Routledge
Taylor & Francis Group

LONDON AND NEW YORK

First published 2022
by Routledge
4 Park Square, Milton Park, Abingdon, Oxon OX14 4RN

and by Routledge
605 Third Avenue, New York, NY 10158

Routledge is an imprint of the Taylor & Francis Group, an informa business

British Library Cataloguing-in-Publication Data
A catalogue record for this book is available from the British Library

Library of Congress Cataloging-in-Publication Data
Names: King, Peter, 1960– author.
Title: Speculations on the question: what is housing? / Peter King.
Description: Milton Park, Abingdon, Oxon; New York, NY :
Routledge, 2022. | Includes bibliographical references and index.
Identifiers: LCCN 2021053731 (print) | LCCN 2021053732 (ebook) |
ISBN 9781032244815 (hardback) | ISBN 9781032252773 (paperback) |
ISBN 9781003282457 (ebook)
Subjects: LCSH: Housing policy—Moral and ethical aspects. |
Dwellings.
Classification: LCC HD7287.3.K58 2022 (print) | LCC HD7287.3
(ebook) |DDC 363.5—dc23/eng/20211109
LC record available at https://lccn.loc.gov/2021053731
LC ebook record available at https://lccn.loc.gov/2021053732

ISBN: 978-1-032-24481-5 (hbk)
ISBN: 978-1-032-25277-3 (pbk)
ISBN: 978-1-003-28245-7 (ebk)

DOI: 10.1201/9781003282457

Typeset in Goudy
by codeMantra

As at first, so at the last:
To B, H & R

Contents

x *Contents*

Preface

I wrote this essay in early 2019, several months before I, or, indeed, anyone else, had heard of COVID-19. It might be said then that this essay relates to a more innocent time when we could see dwelling in a rather different light. Indeed, there have been many comments over the last couple of years about the perils of people being stuck at home with the heightened risk of loneliness, depression and domestic abuse. The lockdowns of 2020 and 2021, it might be said, have cast a considerable shadow over the idea of our home as a place of security, comfort and complacency.

Yet, I wrote this piece in the aftermath of a period of considerable difficulty for my family involving a tragedy that we still struggle to come to terms with. There is no mention of this tragedy in what follows (and only the most fleeting of references to the COVID-19 pandemic in a footnote in the final section). I did not at the time, and do not now, see this essay as a response to or in any way directly connected to my family circumstances.

Having completed this essay by the Summer of 2019, and even having let some people read and comment on it, I decided to leave it alone. Being retired, I am under no compulsion to publish and the idea of being quiet for a time had a certain appeal. When the United Kingdom went into lockdown in March 2020, this seemed to justify my hesitancy in trying to have this work published. It was now all too easy to see dwelling as a locus for problems, for harm, rather than anything positive.

Yet, when one thinks about it, that is a very shallow argument. Of course, there are problems with isolation and even violence connected with our private existence. There always have been and unfortunately there probably always will be. The dwelling is not always a place of security and comfort. But if we focus on the problems we lose sight of the reality, and this is, to say it bluntly, that most of time for most of us, dwelling is precisely a place of security and comfort. Churchill famously said that democracy was the worst form of government, except for all the other forms that had been tried from time to time. We can say the something similar about private dwelling: it can be awful until we consider the alternatives. And most of us only have the time and leisure to consider those alternatives because we have somewhere secure and comfortable to go home to.

So in the face of personal tragedy or a pandemic what can we do? We can cry, we can rant and rave and we can bemoan all that is wrong with what we have and where we are. But then what do we do? We carry on, using what we have where we are. And so, it occurs to me now that this essay's merit is precisely in that it makes no mention of the tragic events in my life or the pandemic that has kept so many of us indoors.

*

This essay is not a work of critique and my aim is not to target any particular text, thinker or policy. The work is almost entirely speculative. The anecdotes I have used are entirely from my own personal and professional experience and the references on housing are, with only a few exceptions, all my own books. I have done this for at least two reasons. First, I have taken seriously the notion of writing subjectively on subjectivity. Second, this work is an attempt to think further on concepts I have developed in the past. I consider that these concepts have considerable explanatory power and so I have sought to bring them together and develop them. This work then derives almost entirely from the previous work I have done. I have written much on dwelling in the past. I still feel that this work stands up and says something that is important. This current essay is not then a reconsideration of that work, but an attempt to develop certain aspects of it and to present it in a more condensed yet, I hope, developed manner based on a further 15 years of thinking and lived experience.

The key difference to my mind is that I have divorced myself as completely as I can from what I have called 'policy thinking' and what its practitioners refer to as 'housing studies'. As will be clear from reading the essay, I insist that what is commonly seen as the field of housing is both misnamed and misdirected. I have sought, therefore, to free my thinking from these ideas and develop a work that is more consistent with a properly subjective approach, whereby I consider housing exclusively from the inside and not merely as a quantity for the study of policy failure.

As someone who is now outside the academy, I am free to attempt such a work without feeling I have to comply with the consensus, or to compose the work in a manner that conforms to the output culture of UK higher education. I have prepared this work in my own way and it is important to me that it takes this form. I do this positively and without rejecting other equally serious approaches taken by thinkers with differing priorities. And, of course, I lose nothing if everyone else disagrees.

*

I have a number of people to thank for their help and guidance in completing this work. I am grateful to Yoric Irving-Clarke and Helen Taylor for their comments on an earlier draft of the essay. I like to thank the two anonymous reviewers of the manuscript for their comments and support for the work. I am also very appreciative of the support I have received from Ed Needle and his colleagues at Routledge.

My wife, B, has been a constant source of strength, wisdom and sound common sense as well as being my sternest critic, and I could not live without her. My daughters, Helen and Rachel, are a constant source of inspiration as well as now proving to be pretty stern critics themselves.

Finally, when writing this essay in 2019, I intended it as my last words on housing. I am even more certain two years on that this is the case.

Peter King
November 2021

Speculations on the Question: What Is Housing?

The question

The question is: *what is housing?* From this question there naturally proceeds another: *what is not housing?*

The basic distinctions I wish to draw here are between inside and outside, inclusion and exclusion, between care for and cares of. I contrast housing as dwelling with housing as policy thinking.

I seek to place a boundary around housing. I undertake my study from inside this boundary, within dwelling, within what I take housing to be.

I choose to leave what is outside – what is not housing – where it lies.

Writing subjectively on the subjective

When we think and write about the use of dwelling, we find that we focus on the actions we undertake and not the object containing them. Dwelling is not an object we hold. It holds us. And, this allows us to look elsewhere. We do not focus on housing when we are using it. We do not spend our time observing and commenting on it, looking at the décor or comparing it with other dwellings. We use the fridge and washbasin and do not look at them as distinct objects every time we approach them. We focus on what matters to us while relying on the utility of the fridge and the washbasin. We can do this because this place and the things in it are just where we expect them to be. These things remain in place. So, when we focus on the use of housing, the last thing we consider is the brick box and certainly not the means we have for accessing it and paying for it. Dwelling only works when we can take all this for granted.

And, this means that when we write about dwelling as it is used, we should likewise expect it – the object – to disappear as we focus on the

DOI: 10.1201/9781003282457-1

singularity of our use of what are subsidiary elements to fulfilling our interests. In attending to the use of our dwelling, we lose sight of it as the object that encloses this subjective experience. We stop looking at the dwelling and focus on what we do inside it. When we are using our dwelling, it becomes opaque to our consciousness. Housing is just the background. It is just as necessary – we cannot live without it – but we do not live for it.

We have to take very seriously the fact that the use of dwelling takes place behind closed doors and with the curtains drawn. It is not meant to be observed and reduced to calculation. It is private and only operates when it remains so. To open it up to public scrutiny is to destroy what makes dwelling work.

But how then can we think and write about it properly? Can we ever get to the subjective without destroying it? How can we describe what cannot be observed publicly? Perhaps we can never do it fully, and for some, this might mean we should not even try.

However, I want to suggest a way in which we can address the subjective appreciation of dwelling in a manner that retains its essential subjectivity. We can do it simply by focusing on how we – and I mean here the particular thinker and writer – use our dwelling. In other words, the way to properly appreciate the subjective use of dwelling is by describing and analysing how I use my own dwelling and what happens as a result of this use.[1]

The subjective, so to speak, is not merely within us: we are within it. We can never get outside of it or beyond it. We can either accept the subjective or continue with our delusions. But these delusions do not take us out of the subjective. The subjective focuses on what is meaningful to us rather than what is merely quantifiable. It relates to the specificity of

---

1 I can imagine there will be an immediate response to this statement along the lines that this is a white middle-class male view. I want to deal briefly with that objection. Any such statement carries within it the assumptions that simply stating the view that the author belongs to a particular subset of society makes them representative of that group. The effect of this labelling then is to devalue or discredit their argument without having actually to engage with the detail of it. The author is simply guilty of whatever vices that particular subset is prey to. It is assumed that membership of this subset determines one's thoughts and actions, so allowing identification of membership of that subset to determine the response needed to whatever argument they might put forward. But to hold these two assumptions about members of this sub-set is, of course, to fall foul of these assumptions oneself. How does the reader know the author is typical of this sub-set unless the reader is already carrying within them a set of deterministic presuppositions? Therefore, the proper response to those who insist on pigeonholing an author as representative of a particular set of views is to politely request that they first examine their own prejudices and, having cleared their minds of these, then get on with the business of reading what is there rather than what they presume to be present.

things we use rather than what is general and standardised. It helps us focus on quality rather than merely concerning ourselves with what is measurable. As such, to deny the subjective is to empty the world of all that is meaningful to us. It takes away love, caring, solidarity, altruism, affection and emotion.

In emphasising the subjective, I do not wish to assert that there is no objective world independent of our experience of it. There is an objective world, but we can never experience it as purely objective. There is a tendency to see the subjective and objective as opposites that are mutually exclusive, where being objective means that we reject the subjective. But this is too simplistic. There is a place for a cold and value-free examination of the object world. But we do not want this always or even most of the time. Detached examination should be reserved for particular occasions that call for the disinterested observer. But most of the time, in our relations with others, in the setting of our personal goals and in our relations with things close to us, an entirely or even predominantly objective approach would be counter-productive and even harmful. It is the difference between falling in love with that one particular person and going in search of a mate.

Where the objective dominates, there is a tendency to downgrade those elements of our lives that really matter and carry the greatest weight. We put these at the periphery by focusing on what can be quantified as if the process by which we garner knowledge is more important than the knowledge itself. But in doing so, we tend to forget that subjectivity is the default position for most of us, most of the time. It is the objective gaze that is the aberration from the norm, the oddity. Real life, what we commonly call 'lived experience', is subjective. Reality is determined by the subjective. Real life is where we make no attempt to control the variable, perhaps where we do not even recognise that there are variables to control.

But we can go further. We cannot devise a statement on the importance of the objective without relating it to the subjective. Any such statement must ultimately rest on a subjective interpretation, belief or claim based on some thought that either we have had ourselves or taken in and then interpreted. There is simply no way in which we can assert that a belief or thought has been derived objectively. For example, we might suggest that logical positivism, which denies meaning to any question incapable of verification, is itself based on subjective assumptions about the nature of the world and its meaningfulness.

It is fair to say that no one goes so far as to deny the existence of the subjective. What tends to happen though is attempts to control it, limit it and bind it by objective criteria. The subjective can be studied by some externally verifiable means that open it up to measurement. But we might ask, is the decision to control the subjective and rely solely or mainly on objective criteria itself an objective decision? On what basis do we decide on the necessity of the objective? The limits of the objective are determined subjectively and this, of course, means that the limits of the subjective themselves are not objective. This is not to say that our mind is closed off to the external. The point is rather that we can only view the world through a subjective lens.

We presume that the objective is the same for everyone, but we know that facts are often disputed. We know that the apparently objective is not immune to conflict and differing interpretations. This is because we each perceive what we take to be objective very differently. In other words, we view it subjectively.

Indeed, subjectivity is not necessarily distinct from rationality. One can be rational and subjective. We should see rationality as a process – the means by which we determine what action it would be reasonable for us to take. But we start from a particular set of beliefs or reasons, which can be derived either objectively or subjectively. In this regard, rationality can be the tool of our subjectivity. Subjectivity need not be woolly and imprecise. There can be a rigour in self-examination and reflection. We can be hard on ourselves. Indeed, only we can be truly hard on ourselves. We cannot hide things from ourselves in the manner we can from other people.

The difficulty for any subjective approach is that there can be no unmediated external access to the subject. The subjective can only ever be known to *that* subject. What someone else thinks and feels and so takes as meaningful about their dwelling, or anything else, cannot be known directly by anyone else. This knowledge cannot be transferred without using language (or some other medium such as pictures) and the ability of the subject to articulate what is inside them accurately and correctly (and what possible way have we of determining accuracy and correctness here?). The external observer has to trust what the subject says about the state of their thoughts and feelings and be able to interpret them in a manner that has a high degree of commonality with the subject. We have to know that we both mean the same thing and we can never be sure of this.

Yet we also have to admit that we share the same mental equipment. Each of us is a thinking human subject. We have a self, a mind, a consciousness or whatever we might choose to call it. We are the same in terms of our biology, psychology and brain chemistry and general capacity to learn. In other words, we have similar hardware and software, even if it might operate more or less effectively in each of us. The fact that we can learn language, talk to and understand each other is absolutely fundamental here. We all have similar emotions and anxieties. We show anger, joy, lust and passion, which are all generated internally and which act on us distinctly. No one in this sense is unique and so there is every reason to suggest that we are using the same processes and going through the same operations as everyone else. Admittedly, we can only surmise this, but it is reasonable to do so.

This means that when I write about my subjective experience of dwelling, about what it means to live with those I choose to share my life with, in an enclosed space where all others are excluded, I can have a degree of confidence that it will resonate with others. They may not agree with some or all of my reasoning or my conclusions, but they will be able to recognise, in general terms, the place from which I am arguing. This is because they too occupy a similar subjective space with those they choose to include in their exclusive domain. We can then make comparisons based on this mutual familiarity with private space, even though each private space remains opaque to any external and supposedly objective gaze. This then provides us with the possibility of making statements about how we use dwelling and what it may mean to us. We will not be able to weigh or measure these statements. We can merely compare them with statements and descriptions made by others concerning their private dwelling. But the fact that we all share this common activity of private dwelling makes comparison not only possible but meaningful.

Having established an approach, I now turn to the substantive purpose of this essay. Much of the discussion here is on what I refer to as dwelling. It is an understanding of this concept which will help answer my initial question. But I wish to begin by considering what housing is not, with what I see as the fundamental problem that has to be dealt with before we can fully appreciate what housing is.

Policy thinking

Can we properly study the lack of something without fully appreciating what that something is and does? But this is precisely what the field of academic research commonly called 'housing studies' does. Within this field, most of what properly constitutes housing are taken for granted and left largely unanalysed. The field tends only to look at problems and exceptions, at those issues that are outside of the standard experience of housing that most people, including the researchers themselves, currently experience. Looking at a much better-established area of research, it would be like medical students ignoring a typical human body and only studying decayed and damaged corpses on the assumption that this is how the body is supposed to be. We would not study human anatomy using only seriously damaged car crash victims, so why try to understand housing by its exceptions?

What is being studied in the field of housing studies is not housing as such. Rather it is the study of the failure of policy. Accordingly, I refer to this activity as *policy thinking* to differentiate it from the rest of the work here which concerns itself more properly with what I take housing to be. I wish to insist that we make a clear and thorough distinction between policy thinking, on the one hand, and private dwelling, on the other hand. Indeed, I want to go as far as to suggest that these two areas of study are really looking at completely different things. I can demonstrate this with another comparison. Those who are interested in healthy eating might focus on one of two things. First, they may be concerned with nutrition and what effect certain food groups have on human health and well-being. They study human metabolism and it is affected by certain types of foods. This might extend to looking at the ways in which the consumption of certain food might be encouraged or discouraged. Second, one might be interested in the production and distribution of food and how individual households can access it. In other words, this is the study of food production, supply chains and affordability. Both of these types of study are necessary, but they are also clearly different in the concepts they develop, the manner in which research is undertaken and the types of skills needed by researchers. My argument is that what is called housing studies or housing research is akin to the second type of study. It is akin to analysing supermarket supply chains and considering whether the food sold is affordable to all households. But there is no attempt to look at what impact these products have on those that use them. Housing studies – or more properly, policy thinking – only look at production, distribution and affordability and have no concern for use, for what happens on the other side of the front door. It has developed a number of means of undertaking these studies, but these are of no help to us once we start to analyse what is happening on the other side of the door. Put simply then, policy thinking and private dwelling are completely different subjects and should be seen as such.

Policy thinking is the study of the failure of policy, not housing as such. It studies how the policy process fails, where objectives are missed, and perhaps goes on to try to understand why this might have occurred. However, this thinking does not have anything to do with housing. Housing is not what we are told it is by those who claim expertise in policy thinking. What they are expert in is not housing but policy failure. Housing is purely incidental to this and is merely the quantity that defines the failure of policy.

Of course, why policy fails is important, and it should be studied. But, to reiterate, *it is not housing.* Policy thinking could be concerned with any area of public policy. It could look at why policies in education, health, aviation or military procurement fail. All these areas use the same basic approach, based on a similar literature and common methods. The aim is to understand the policy process and why it goes wrong. Certainly, policy thinking on housing feels the need for some understanding of housing. It will have to be aware of key terminology, some of the history of provision that has led to this point (in other words, past policy failure), the organisation of institutions and relevant legislation. But the actual techniques of the study of policy failure are not dependent on any specific housing knowledge. Housing could be replaced by aviation without any basic change in the structure or approach of the study.

The problem for policy thinking is precisely that *housing works.* Generally speaking, housing does what it should, and this means that any study of housing is inevitably the study of private dwelling: the study of comfort, security and complacency (King, 2004, 2005, 2008, 2017a). But this is less dramatic, less unpredictable and less prone to change than the drama around policy failure. It appears to demand merely a description of private dwelling as it is. There is no predetermined necessity to change or reform what happens in private dwelling. We can merely observe what is happening and try to determine its meaning. Such a study is essentially qualitative and, as I have stated above, dependent on a subjective appreciation of how private dwelling might be used. What it does not allow for is a ready prescription for change or any possibility of measurable outcomes. We might further add that private dwelling provides no justification for radicalism (apart, of course, from providing radicals with a comfortable and secure place to hide).

This situation is seemingly unacceptable to policy thinking. It does not wish to focus on what it thinks of as mundane and without consequence. Instead, it chooses to look at two main areas. First, it focuses on *quantities,* such as the levels of building and finance within a particular domain; the standards of dwellings within this domain (in comparison to the past, other domains or some more abstract measure) and matters of finance, particularly how much would be needed to meet a particular quantity of housing at a given standard. This quantitative thinking might be extended to looking at the levels of income needed by certain groups to gain access to housing of the appropriate standard within the domain. Inevitably, the focus of such studies will be on aggregates – populations or parts thereof, costings and budgets, etc. – and be statistically based allowing for ready measurement of the extent of policy failure (King, 1996). But because it is largely statistical, there will be a tendency to focus on the outliers and exceptions rather than the norms.

This, then, brings us to the second focus of policy thinking. Policy thinking, driven by the quantitative, will tend to focus only on the *exceptions*. It will look at issues such as homelessness, access and affordability, and light on disasters should they occur. It is always tempting to focus on the exceptions. After all, it is apparently where the problems that need solving are. In comparison, there is the habitual, mundane and ordinary use of private dwelling. Compared to the exceptions and crises identified by policy thinking, ordinary use is apparently inconsequential. There is nothing exciting, there is no drama or change. No particular event in ordinary use seems to have an impact and every day is like any other. Nothing seems to matter.

But this focus on the exceptional offers a fundamentally skewed vision of how housing works. In fact, it looks at the very opposite, where housing does not work. Focusing on how housing does not work at best only references implicitly what housing does. It examines housing only as a lack or an absence. Policy thinking then studies what housing is not, what it does not do. It seems to take for granted the virtues of housing – its core function, meaning and purpose – and studies only its abstract provision and cost, or their absence. We only learn what housing does by default. But this is despite the fact that an overwhelming majority of the population experience housing not as an absence but as a satisfying presence. Accordingly, the inevitable outcome of policy thinking is the denigration of the very entity that the researchers purport to be concerned with. Housing as private dwelling, that which shelters us and allows us to live secure and comfortable lives, is deemed to be a perversion. Instead, policy thinking studies the absence of housing *as caused by policy*. The result is the normalisation of the exception and hence the idea of a permanent housing crisis as a representation of the ongoing moral imperative towards the exception. Perversely though, this merely perpetuates the crisis – or at least the rhetoric of crisis – it being now a natural part of the system with rules devised explicitly for it.

Policy thinking uses the exceptional – where housing does not work as we would expect – to frame the general rules about housing. It seeks to do this in the name of inclusivity, but this tends to have the reverse effect in that it provides the excluded with every incentive to remain outside. This is precisely because the rules only apply to those excluded. Focusing on the exceptions institutionalises their difference from the majority and so maintains it. It normalises the exceptions by giving them a moral force, which, in turn, delegitimises the majority, and hence the use of terms such as 'commodification' to refer to the main means we have of accessing housing. The aim of the term is to question the process as one that is unnatural and a perversion of the norm. The result of this is entirely predictable. The maintaining of separation between the exceptions and the majority alienates the latter and creates an antipathy towards the former. While this serves to reinforce the rhetoric of policy thinking in normalising the exceptions, it does not create any sense of mutuality and common feeling. It does not build anything that could remotely be termed 'social'. The majority feel attacked for not thinking and acting as the exceptions are supposed to do. There is no attempt at acceptance here – no attempt at mutuality – but rather an insistence on obedience and compliance with the rules created by policy thinking. There has then to be a policing function to restrain the alienation of the majority such that policy becomes a matter of enforcement. These so-called norms have to be imposed precisely because they are outside of the ordinary experience of the majority, as it is a consequence of policy thinking to institutionalise the divisions between exceptions and the majority.

This is all done supposedly on behalf of the exceptions. However, the exceptions are themselves defined by policy thinking and are not self-identified. They too fall prey to the resulting rigidities, which appear to make a virtue of their exceptionalism. We can say then that policy thinking leads to the creation of rules that deny any mutuality and accommodation. They deny the possibility of community by their very attempts to create communities based on standardised notions of quantity and exception.

It does, of course, seem moral to focus on the exceptions rather than the comfortable majority. There is a moral imperative to help those in need. But it does this not in a neutral manner, but by denying any legitimacy to the actions of the majority. There is no study of the majority. They are, so to speak, excluded from policy thinking by dint of their apparent refusal to fail.

What is fascinating is that the creation of this norm flies in the face of the lived experience of its proponents, who are almost all comfortable and outside of the exceptional categories they have devised for others. It is perhaps only possible to undertake policy thinking from a position of comfort, where one is currently free from existential threats and able to look beyond one's immediate needs. Their dwelling works for them, giving them the time and opportunity to think. Their stable systems of care allow them to define, analyse and seek to address unstable systems of care suffered by others.

We might ask where this focus for thinking comes from. Perhaps the predominant reason is one we have already alluded to, namely the fact that the exception is more dramatic and interesting than the norm. Dwelling is dull, regular and perhaps rather boring when it works properly. The consequence is that the dull regularity of private dwelling is excluded and instead policy thinking exceptionalises, focusing on the problems and fetishising them into a permanent crisis. This is done without reference to personal lived experience, which is bracketed out in the name of objectivity. This focus then becomes self-reinforcing over time. The community of policy thinkers talks to itself, and self-selects its norms and modes of discourse, excluding those that challenge it unduly. I do not presume that this process is a calculated one. It is not a deliberate attempt to confound or cynically manipulate. Rather it is based on genuine concern and a need for a sufficient body of research, which, in turn, is reinforced by networking and rhetoric.

One key element of this rhetoric is the belief that the social is morally superior to the individual. To focus on the individual use of dwelling – often referred to as the privatisation or commodification of housing – is seen as regressive and backward, while the social is presumed to be progressive and inclusive. One can speculate as to why this concern for the social is so taken for granted. It is certainly seen as a more sophisticated approach, with individualist explanations taken to be simplistic, or as merely representative of vested interests. In response to this, we might suggest that it is quite frankly absurd to conflate all subjective use into one generalised notion, whether it be class, gender or culture, and posit this as an explanatory improvement on the vast diversity of individual use across time and space. Perhaps the reason that social explanations are taken to be more sophisticated is as banal as the fact that individualist or liberal explanations preceded social ones – or maybe staying outside dwelling is simply safer and easier to deal with. It allows for quantification, which is both convenient and capable of being classed as science. In policy thinking, things become real only when they can be counted.

But whatever the reason, the focus on the social makes it impossible to focus on the use of dwelling, and this is because use is *never* social. Our use of dwelling is always individualised and privatised and cannot be anything else while remaining dwelling. Dwelling does involve shared practices which, it might be argued, are culturally conditioned. But dwelling is always experienced individually and as *mine*.[2] Hence the focus on the social stops at the front door and is confounded by the private activity of dwelling as exclusive use.

---

2 In my book *In Dwelling* (King, 2008) and here, I use the term *mine* (always italicised) not to denote those things that belong to me personally (I would use the term in its non-italicised form were I doing this), but to refer to the sense of possessive closeness that individuals have to things with which they have a legitimate exclusive relation, those things taking on their meaning precisely because they are personally held. In other contexts, this sense of *mine* can also refer to our relations with other people.

The success of policy thinking is in its ability to move from one apparent consensus to another without consequence and without any apparent need to dwell on any self-contradiction this might involve. What matters for the policy thinker is not the correctness of one's thinking, there being no consequences for wrong judgements or conclusions, but in never being left behind or caught out thinking the wrong thing. Policy thinking thrives by replacing the possibility of critique with the necessity of consensus. It insists on a uniformity of purpose.

What sustains policy thinking in this is speed. It moves quickly from one issue to another. In this way, the consequences of failure do not have to be dealt with. What matters is that one is facing the current urgent issue and one has no time to deal with what is now in the past. The 'next thing' always allows the policy thinker to be positive, move forward and ignore past failures without consequence. Indeed to draw attention to failure is seen as negative and deemed to be cynical and unhelpful.

Policy thinking is where too much is considered possible, where aspiration is taken as normal and where we expect to expand, to go beyond the threshold of dwelling. Dwelling is always being forced outwards, as if to create something larger and more significant. However, significance must be measurable and so thinking is restricted to the quantitative. This means that policy thinking is necessarily external to dwelling. Its purpose is to process dwelling as a quantity, and so, it must generate its purpose from outside of dwelling. Policy thinking takes dwelling for granted, but not in a positive sense. It does not treat dwelling as habitual, but merely as uninteresting and non-controversial. It considers that there is nothing to be said, but only things to be counted. There is nothing tacit or habitual in policy thinking. Indeed, it seeks to break habits and enforce new patterns. It is based on a presumption of improvement and development and, most worryingly, the idea that dwelling in itself is not enough.

Of course, policy thinking sees no problem here. It is not aware of what it lacks. This is precisely because it is outside of dwelling. But it is not just a matter of being ignorant of what dwelling is. Policy thinking genuinely thinks it can and does know. How else could it deem itself able to 'make policy'?

Policy thinking likes to talk about the commodification of housing. There tend to be arguments in favour of *de*commodification, which is seen as a good thing, and criticism of apparent *re*commodification, which is never described as a good thing. For policy thinking, the enemy is 'the market', and the aim of policy is to take housing off the market.

This, it seems to me, is an entirely good idea: we should seek ways of taking housing out of market relations. However, this is not to be done through the socialisation of housing, which merely replaces the market with another value system that can be equally as arbitrary. The proper way to take housing off the market is to focus on personal use. The only way we can 'decommodify' housing is through concentrating on the way we use our own dwelling and so stop seeing it as a commodity. We can ignore the asset value, costs and debt and use dwelling as a benign tool, as a means to fulfil our self-defined ends. In this way of thinking, we see dwelling as an activity and not as an asset to hold. Dwelling need have no price tag as far as we are concerned, and of course, in most cases, this is the case. We take our housing out of the market by simply closing the door. The dwelling stops being an object and becomes a tool: dwelling stops being a noun and becomes a verb.

Taking the term literally, only a very tiny fraction of dwellings are ever 'on the market' at any one time, and in the lifetime of an individual dwelling, it is only for sale for a short period of its long life. For most of us, most of the time, the very idea of the market does not enter our dwelling.

Most of us, most of the time, do not want our dwelling to be on the market because it quite fundamentally alters it for us. We start to think about the dwelling as a distinct physical object, and in particular, how it appears or might appear to potential buyers. What do others think of it? Is it desirable? Can we get the asking price? If I spend £X on improvements, can I get £2X extra on the sale price? The dwelling becomes an object and starts to grow more distant from us. It becomes a distinct thing that we are forced to observe dispassionately.

Clearly, in most cases, we have chosen to put the house up for sale. It may no longer suit our purposes or aspirations, or we may need to move to somewhere else for work. But the sale may also be forced due to such things as financial problems or relationship breakdown. Whatever the reason though, once we put the dwelling on the market, we start to separate the object from our use of it, and our use changes in order to maintain and increase the presumed value of the dwelling. We feel that we must only use the dwelling in a certain way in order to protect it. As a result, our use becomes contingent and our actions conscious and deliberate. We do not wish to burden the dwelling or impose upon it and so detract from its value. We wish to show it off as we perceive others might wish it to be, rather than how we want it. Dwelling becomes performative rather than habitual. It is no longer ours in the same way, but it takes on a life beyond our use of it.

It is a time when our use of dwelling becomes open to judgement. We show the place off to others for them to judge it. Within our own dwelling, we become beholden to others, who view it and, implicitly, our use of it. We of course have done this too when deciding on whether to purchase a dwelling lived in by someone else.

We cannot 'de-marketise' housing as such, but we can keep our dwelling off the market, and we do this most of the time without having to make any special effort. We decommodify dwelling simply by ignoring its market value, by, day to day, seeing its asset value as a matter of complete indifference to us. More generally, the more we think about dwelling as an activity rather than policy thinking, then the less we will commodify housing. Housing is only commodified by the way we think about it. Focusing on the internal and ignoring the external will help us here.

Most of the time, housing only has a use value – and the very idea of 'value' here is not one we would choose to use ourselves, any more than we actively think of our habitual use. We might argue that those without housing are not indifferent to use value, but the proper issue here is whether they wish to be indifferent or not. They would dearly wish to fall into habitual use of dwelling. That some are poorly housed should not be taken as a reason to dismiss the aim of what dwelling exists to do and would allow these households to do as soon as they were well-housed.

What we consider housing to be is alien to the consensus of policy thinking. Housing is an activity within a boundary that excludes unwanted others and so include those that we care for. This is housing not as policy thinking but as dwelling, and it is to this that we now turn our focus.

Private dwelling

The word dwelling, like housing, can be used both as a noun and a verb. It can be used to refer to a unit of residential accommodation or the activity, or series of activities, generally defined as living in a settled and permanent manner. But dwelling used as a noun is profoundly different from its use as a verb. As a noun, it is formal and used as a technical term. This is because it is seen as neutral and capable of denoting any form of residential space, be it a house, flat, bungalow or mobile home. It is used because it is non-specific and impersonal, telling us nothing about the nature of the accommodation except that it is used as residential accommodation. Dwelling as a noun is used because it is inclusionary.

However, dwelling as a verb is much less formal, less precise and, therefore, rather harder to define. It has no hard technical definition that allows it to be used with the specificity of dwelling as a noun. It can encompass the most public to most private, from the very idea of human settlement to the private household separating itself from all others. We can also say that dwelling as a verb is exclusionary in that, while it can refer to space at all levels from the most public to most private, it is always concerned with boundaries, with delimiting space to allow it to be used by some group whether it be a nation or a household.

Martin Heidegger, in his essay 'Building, Dwelling, Thinking' (1971), equates dwelling with building: for humans to dwell means that they build structures for themselves. In turn, he defines building, through its etymological roots in Old English and German, as related to the verb 'to remain' or 'to stay in place' (Heidegger, 1971, p. 146). Dwelling as building is, thus, more than mere shelter but is a reference to the settlement by human beings on the earth. Indeed, for Heidegger, dwelling is humanity's 'being on the earth' (p. 147). Dwelling is the house, the village, the town, the city and the nation in their generality. It is the gathering of humans into meaningful commitment with their environment.

According to Christian Norberg-Schulz (1985), dwelling refers to spaces and places, both in terms of how they are used and what this use means to individuals and communities. He suggests that dwelling can mean three things. First, it involves meeting others for the exchange of products, ideas and feelings, where life is experienced as a multitude of possibilities. It is where we come together socially and economically. Second, dwelling means accepting a set of common values. It is through this that we can share. We dwell through establishing and operating conventions. Dwelling is here seen as moral and political and engendering civil relationships. Third, Norberg-Schulz states that dwelling is where we can be ourselves, where we have a small chosen world of our own. It is our private place where we can withdraw from the wider world. It is this third sense that I wish to focus on in this essay and so when I am discussing dwelling, I am invariably referring to it as private dwelling. Yet it is important to remember that private dwelling is an activity nested within something that is much larger.

But before focusing on private dwelling there is a further general point to be made. In 'Building, Dwelling, Thinking' (1971), Heidegger states that dwelling 'remains for man's everyday experience that which is from the outset "habitual"'... For this it recedes behind the manifold ways in which dwelling is accomplished' (p. 147). Heidegger sees dwelling as habitual. It is the implicit, familiar, seemingly unchanging routine of habit. But more than this, it is hidden from consciousness behind the varied ways in which it is undertaken and achieved. Our ordinary experience, which is itself dwelling, hides the significance of dwelling from us. We are too busy dwelling to see the full significance of what these very acts enclose.

We say that we inhabit a place, and this habitation is formed by the activity of dwelling. Inhabiting can be seen as bringing our habits into a place. We populate the place with our habits and it becomes inhabited once this is attained.

Private dwelling can be defined as *protected intimacy* (Bachelard, 1969). It is where we feel we reside in a bounded space that is secure, comfortable and private and where we are in control of who to include and exclude. Private dwelling is the confinement of intimacy by boundaries and mutual indifference, where we see indifference as the benign state in which we inadvertently ignore all others through focusing on those that are close to us. This is admittedly quite a complex set of concepts that have been linked together, as yet without any explanation. While the rest of this essay seeks to unpack these concepts and expand on this definition of private dwelling, for the moment, we might settle on a rather more straightforward concept and suggest that dwelling is simply what we do when we use the object we call a dwelling. Accordingly, in referring to dwelling, we should see it always as both a noun and a verb together, as both an object and an activity. Therefore, throughout this essay, I do not so much use the word interchangeably but concurrently. It is always already a verb and a noun. The activity is always wrapped up in the object.

Private dwelling is the manifestation of settlement most relevant to our ordinary lives. We return to the same place every time and it is reasonable to expect that we will continue to do so into the future. We live with the same people for an extended period of time and it is reasonable to expect that we will continue to do so as well. So, we expect our dwelling to be permanent and predictable, where any change is discretionary and it is reasonable to expect it will continue to be so. This place we return to and share is then known to us and as such we are able to use it without conscious engagement.

For most of us, most of the time (and this holds throughout human history), dwelling has always already been provided. We were literally born into it. Dwelling is already there, and we learn to dwell fully just as we learn to walk and speak our native language. We arrived into the world already within dwelling. It is the fundamental condition of our existence. As such, we can safely take it for granted and carry on with the illusion that we can make our own place in the world.

Dwelling behaves

We dwell because of the elements and other people. We dwell to be in contact with particular others in a way that allows us to control and limit our contact with everyone else. We need to exclude because, while we can take dwelling for granted, we cannot, and should not, take others for granted.

We need to be able to take this capability to exclude for granted, so as not to continually cause offence. Dwelling allows us to forget that we are not alone and we need to be with others.

Dwelling is an activity, but no dwelling is active. It is an activity that depends on the passivity of its object. Dwelling comforts us by being hard and unyielding. We know it will not give way. I trust that my dwelling will behave and will continue to work as it should. Even when it rains constantly for three or four days, there are no leaks, but I would not expect there to be any. It can be freezing outside, but nothing freezes inside and nor should anything. It can be blowing a gale, but the dwelling stands fast. The dwelling stands and holds us tight.

This is most assuredly nothing special. It is precisely what a modern dwelling is designed to do, and for most of them, most of the time, it is precisely what they do. But is it not remarkable that it does? And is it not equally remarkable that we expect it to, such that we need not even think about how remarkable it is? No dwelling need work well. There is so much that can go wrong and, of course, sometimes things do go wrong: dwellings can leak, be too cold or be structurally unsound.

However, most dwellings do not leak; they are warm and are structurally sound. This should matter to us, not because we are cruel or ignorant of any lack that some households might have. But it should matter because this is how housing is most of the time and how we want housing to be all of the time. This is what housing is for and exactly how it ought to be. We do not expect dwelling to let us down, and by and large it does not.

Most of us live in situations of non-decision. It is not that we cannot decide – there is no indecision – but that we have nothing of any real import that needs a decision. We might have to choose what to have for breakfast, what shoes to wear and what to watch on TV, but we have nothing of consequence to detain us and, furthermore, we do not expect anything to crop up. This does not mean that crises will not happen or that things will not go wrong. Rather it is that mostly things do not go wrong, and from experience, we know that tomorrow is very likely to be like today and last week and the week before that.

Dwelling offers us the space within which to move and grow. It is not a perfect fit and so we can move around within it and develop and shape ourselves according to our own ideals, even where those ideals may be opposed to the manner in which we use dwelling. We can retain the comfort and security of dwelling even when we decry comfort and security and focus on its lack in situations other than ours. Dwelling allows us to think differently from how we act within dwelling. Its passivity and implacability shield us rather than challenge us for our impertinence in plotting against it. Dwelling means we do not have to practise what we preach, and no one need to know and certainly no one has the right to contest how we live. Dwelling can keep us secure even from our own consciences and contradictions. We can carry on deluding ourselves and others because no one gets inside unless we let them. The mismatch between our public and private selves is masked by the privacy of dwelling itself. Dwelling means that we need not sacrifice anything for our beliefs.

Dwelling helps us remain unaware of many things. It can mean we never have to face a stranger. Dwelling can mean that everyone else is a stranger. Dwelling can mean that we know no one. Dwelling can mean that no one knows we know no one. Dwelling means that strangers can continue to ignore us with a clear conscience. They need not know that we exist.

Machines and organisms

I was lying in bed on a Thursday morning just before Easter, with no plans other than to roll over. It was too early to get out of bed, and I had nothing to get up early for. As planned, at 7.00 am, the heating system clicked into life with its distinctive rumble and low hum. Usually, this is a comforting noise, suggesting that things are working as they should. Except that they did not continue to work as they should on this morning. The low hum was replaced by a clang as if someone had dropped their tools on the landing, and then a loud bang. There was still a humming but louder and more insistent with an ominous edge. There was also a smell of burning. The heating pump had burnt out after more than 20 years of consistent use. We turned the system off, rang up British Gas and arranged for an engineer to call to replace the pump, which duly happened the following morning. Only the previous week we had been bemoaning the cost of the service agreement with British Gas and wondering if it was worth the expense. Now we were relieved we would be treated as a priority and have the repair done without any unplanned expenditure.

The repair was straightforward and took barely an hour. The real issue for me, however, was the quick shift between the internal and the external, from the interior to the exterior, from the mental to the material. We had no choice but to focus on the physical and the practical, and to look outside for a remedy. With this rapid shift came a mild, but still noticeable, degree of anxiety: what might have happened if we had not been in when the system started up, say if it had been early evening when we are often not in? What if the airing cupboard, full of towels and sheets, had caught fire? More prosaically, would the repair be straightforward? What inconvenience would it involve? Would the engineer turn up as arranged?

It also became clear that there were things in our dwelling that we could not control and could not maintain ourselves. We can use them properly, as we did, but they will still break down in time. There are a number of complex machines in our dwelling that we rely on, that we expect to work reliably and constantly. But we cannot understand them, and we, therefore, have to call on others to come and fix or replace them for us. What we assume will work all the time, because it very nearly does, might not always work. Things can go wrong, and given enough time and use, they will. We had effectively insured against this with our service agreement, and that brought peace of mind, but this does not take anything away from the anxiety of noticing the things around us now as discrete objects and not as anonymous parts of the complex that is dwelling.

I do not as a rule think often about central heating pumps. I do not know how they work and why they break, where to get a new one and how much they cost, or how to replace one. I know that one is needed if the system is to work, and I know where the pump is situated as part of that system. I know how to turn it on and off. But I cannot fix it and I do not really want to learn. I have other priorities than learning plumbing and wiring. Indeed, what I want more than anything is to be able to ignore my central heating pump while it works continually and reliably day after day, month after month and year after year. There are many other complex machines in proximity to me and I understand them no better than the central heating pump. I expect all of these to work reliably for as long as possible. I expect consistency from the complex of machines that contribute to my dwelling such that I can ignore them.

Naturally, when one considers the idea of machines in this context, one's mind goes to Le Corbusier's statement that 'A house is a machine for living in' (Le Corbusier, 1927, p. 95). I have written before on this concept and been critical of the ideas running behind Le Corbusier's statement.[3] Indeed, my continued antipathy towards the notion of the house as machine led me to consider what the opposite might be: if the house is not a machine, then what is it? However, I now considered this question in the context of having to deal with a machine in my house that had decided not to do what it should.

Clearly, the notion of 'the machine' has some pertinence to dwelling. But what might it be? In *In Dwelling*, I defined a machine as:

> An assembly of components so as to perform a particular task, usu-
> ally powered by some means, such as electricity; an apparatus using or

---

3 See King (2008, ch. 3).

applying mechanical power, having several parts each with a definite function and together performing certain kinds of work; an instrument that transmits a force or directs its application.

(King, 2008, p. 47)

A house can certainly be seen as 'an assembly of components', as 'having several parts each with a definite function and together performing certain kinds of work'. It does then look like a machine. But then, the house – the brick box – is not the same as dwelling (King, 2004). Dwelling is more than a unit of accommodation.

We can see this when we consider where Le Corbusier derived his inspiration for his 'machines for living in'. This was the uniformity of modern industry: the factory, the grain silo, the aeroplane and the motor car (Le Corbusier, 1927, 1929). He wished to impose an industrial aesthetic on dwelling. His vision was for mass housing developments where any dwelling 'cell' (as he tellingly referred to them) was to be the same as any other. Any of these 'cells' would do for the modern household. There was to be nothing specific or particular, nothing individual, about any 'cell'. Le Corbusier relished the uniformity of industry, its mass scale and its inherent conformity.

But we just do not see dwelling like that. When we get to the level of our connection with a specific place, what stands out is its distinctiveness. It is definitively different from those around it, even if the external appearance is very nearly indistinguishable. We never mistake our neighbour's dwelling for our own, regardless of how similar they might look. A dwelling is always particular to those using it. Its use is always specific and not interchangeable with any other. Our dwelling is not there simply to sustain us – although it must do that – but it acts too as a repository for our life experience and as a store of memory. While on a utilitarian level, any dwelling of a certain level of amenity would suffice, in practice, we want something specific, and so, we can take our identical 'cell' and make it *mine* (King, 2008). It becomes absolutely specific and distinctive. We want to come home.

Our dwelling is then a place that contains machines, but it is not a machine itself. We might see it as an assembly of machines, but it is not merely this. We have to add to this assembly our memories, relationships (past and current), habits, eccentricities and so on. These are the things that we use our dwelling for. They are the essence of what dwelling is and are what the machines are there to serve.

A machine is something that can transmit force. It is powered in some way. But in what way is dwelling 'powered'? There is no obvious power source (as opposed to what powers the machines within dwelling). Dwelling does not move. It appears to be in stasis and as such might be the very opposite of a machine.

But I want to suggest that dwelling does have a motive power, though not a quantifiable one. We can explore this by positing an alternative metaphor, namely that of the *organism*. We can define an organism in a number of ways. We can see it as a living being, as a distinct thing. But we can also see an organism as a system consisting of interdependent parts. As a living being, an organism is contiguous and complete. But it is made up of a number of interdependent elements all with their prescribed function. This makes it sound like a machine, but there is an important difference. Unlike a machine, an organism is something whose motive force comes from within. It is animated from the inside and does not depend on an external power source. So an organism, like a machine, can be seen as a complex or network of things. It too has a material structure with defined parts. But what animates the organism comes from within and is already part of it.

Like the machines in our dwelling, some parts of us as human beings must be in continuous use. We cannot turn them off and remain a viable being. We can appear to be largely idle when we are at rest or asleep, but some of our core functions, such as digestion, respiration and heart function, must continue to operate. These are involuntary, automatic and outside of our conscious control. They operate without our direct involvement. The same applies to our unconscious mind. We cannot control our dreams. We cannot stop them from bursting into our heads, confusing and confounding us, perhaps even frightening us. There are elements then that are always running in the background, which we cannot control and would struggle to inhibit.

It is in this way that we can see dwelling as an organism, as having a number of systems that appear to work independently and outside of our direct control. It might be argued that we should only take this metaphor so far. Unlike our breathing, we can turn the systems in our dwelling off. We can turn up the heating if we are cold or increase the shower temperature. This is certainly true, and we should be careful to not overstretch our metaphors. But we also need to add that, while we can turn machines off or alter their use, we still need them. There is a cost to turning them off and it may be fatal, just as if some of our core bodily functions ceased to work. A metaphor need not be exact to be helpful to us.

Where the metaphor is especially helpful is with relation to the issue of power. What is it that powers an organism? As we have suggested, it is this that differentiates an organism from a machine, and it is this facet that makes the organism a better metaphor for dwelling than the machine.

One way of looking at this issue, as I have done in some detail in *Private Dwelling* (King, 2004), is the idea of *animation*. There appears to be something that animates us. This can be seen as a life force that turns us from simple matter to living beings. We might be able to measure this life force, in indirect ways through pulse, brain wave patterns, respiration and so on, but this is not the force itself. It is not what gives us life, what gives us a mind. This is what distinguishes us most from a machine. It is also what distinguishes dwelling from the machine.

An inanimate object can only operate in a strictly limited way. It can either work in the prescribed manner or not at all. It always does the best it can. It can do no other. It has no will and nor is it prone to mood swings and tantrums. It may appear temperamental, but this will be perfectly explicable in mechanical terms. A machine will work until it is turned off or breaks. The inanimate is implacable and cannot be reasoned with. There is no contingency, variety or diversity in its operation. An object is functionally transparent. What animates the object – what gives it its spirit – is our use of it. We turn it from an object to a tool, into something that is ours and, for as long as we use it well, it is part of us (Heidegger, 1962). And this applies just as much to those machines over which we do not appear to have conscious control. Just as we have parts of our bodies that we expect to work without any conscious engagement with them, so we expect the same of machines. They have been devised precisely so that we do not have to engage directly with them. They are made to work for us and often in a way that is hidden from us. They are programmed to turn on and off and are often placed away from us so that we do not have direct and regular contact with them. In this sense, it might appear that these objects lack meaning in that we do not directly animate them, and certainly it is the case that we relate to them differently. They remain, as it were, strangers to us. However, these machines are in constant use and they perform crucially important tasks such as heating, lighting and supplying hot water (which is why they are pre-programmed and automatic). Their meaning is necessarily implicit. They are the necessary background or framework on which our conscious lives depend. When these machines break, as the central heating pump did, we are brought up short and made to think about the complexity of dwelling. We can no longer ignore all those things hidden behind doors and walls and kept in inaccessible parts of the dwelling. But just as the heart and lungs are integral to us, so are these machines to dwelling. That we do not have to think about them is precisely the point. We are dependent on them, but this dependency does not have to be made explicit. They remain tools just as much as those objects that we actively pick up. We use them and this use makes them opaque.

A machine can only be animated by our use of it. This is not to give it life as such but to share our life with it for as long as we need it to and for as long as it works as we wish it to. We take the machine and use it, and this gives it meaning.

More machines

But some machines are designed to be shown off and noticed, and this is because, we are told, they are doing new things. These are machines that allow us to keep in touch with the dwelling when we are remote from it and allow possible intruders to know that we are in touch. There are other machines that 'learn' our speech patterns and simply act on our commands: we can ask Alexa to make the world go away.

This raises the question of what impact emerging technologies might have on our dwelling? Are devices like Echo and Ring distinctly different from earlier technologies and will they affect how we use dwelling? These devices use Wi-Fi to link our dwelling with the external and also allow us to connect with our dwelling remotely. Ring is a home security product that notifies the householder if someone comes to the door or is in the vicinity of the house. It offers real-time video and audio and so allows one to 'answer' the door even when one is out of the house. We can then keep watch over the dwelling when physically absent provided we have a Wi-Fi signal and a charged phone or tablet. Echo is a hands-free, voice-activated device that connects with the web and compatible devices in the dwelling. These may all still be emerging technologies and some or all of them may just be passing fads. They may, though, prefigure a major shift in the way we use dwelling and that is certainly how they are being promoted. We might see this as part of a move towards the connected dwelling where we can control all aspects of the dwelling from one device and where there is the possibility of devices 'learning' from our behaviour and regulating the dwelling environment accordingly.

This, it would seem, is a case of technology leading use. The technology makes certain actions possible, so they can, and perhaps should, happen. Some may find a certain kudos in being early adopters, while others will wait to verify their obvious utility (if it exists) before committing to them. But whether one now sees them as attractive or not, there had previously been no great call for these technologies, and they had not been developed to meet any pressing need. The demand for them was, and is, latent at best. We might see this as an example of Say's Law, of supply creating its own demand: there is a device available and affordable (to some), and so we use it and now tell ourselves that we need it. The demand, however, did not exist before the invention of the device.

These devices are marketed in terms of the control and flexibility that they allow us. We can be aware of what is happening to our dwelling when we are away. We can alter the dwelling environment as our circumstances change and be in immediate control, even if we are remote from the dwelling. It is convenient that technology takes on the burden for us and perhaps even pre-empts our needs, having learnt how we behave and what are needs apparently are.

At this point, we might ask if these devices do represent a step change, or are they really just a development from existing technologies, such as the thermostat and the timer clock? The fact that these new devices can 'learn' appears to make them different, but they still depend on how they are programmed and how we use them. They may learn from our habits, but they still depend on these habits as dwelling does at present. They depend on the regularity of our use that we have distinct patterns of behaviour. The device learns what we do on certain days and at certain times and reacts accordingly. In this sense, we are merely programming it in a less conscious manner, but we are still doing it just as we might set up the heating clock differently as conditions change with the seasons. The device in no way alters the habitual nature of dwelling and perhaps even embeds it further.

But do these devices make us feel any safer? This presumably is the point of products such as Ring. We can feel more secure about our dwelling and our possessions even when we are away. In one of the adverts for Ring, we see a rather smug householder in a supermarket queue who remotely warns a possible intruder, having been alerted to his presence from an app on his phone. The intruder, surprised and worried that he might be identified, scurries off and the camera returns to the contented householder looking up from his phone. A potential burglary has been prevented, and no nasty surprises await the stout householder on his return home. The device is marketed as preventing crime and giving us peace of mind. Of course, it may just shift the crime to the next house or the next road, but we might not get to know about this, and it is not we who are suffering. So, we can remain smug as we warn the burglar off. If our neighbours had any sense, they would be doing the same as we are and investing in this new gadget.

However, the device connects only to a rather particular notion of safety. We may consider that one of the main aims of a dwelling is to keep *us* safe and secure, protect *us* from the elements and intruders and keep the world at bay. But the issue here is the safety of the dwelling and its physical contents. By definition, we use the device when we are absent and so in no personal danger from intruders. Using a device like Ring suggests that our main concern is with the integrity and safety of the dwelling, preserving it as an asset. We should obviously not dismiss the trauma and sense of violation caused by intrusion and the loss of valuable and familiar items but is Ring nothing more than a possession to help protect our other possessions? Ring protects the things we own, but it does not make *us* safer.

Indeed, we ought to ask whether controlling the dwelling from outside enhances or detracts from private dwelling. We may feel in control, but we have to notice that we are. We cannot take our control for granted. We might even suggest that video security externalises the anxieties that we might have. We take our anxiety with us when we leave, and so get no respite from it, and it only becomes heightened. The device emphasises the notion of dwelling as an asset and not as a tool we use. Accordingly, our use becomes conscious and deliberative. The way the dwelling works as an object becomes more transparent to us and more obviously contingent by being so overtly linked to technology. It heightens the sense of dwelling as an end in itself rather than as a means.

Using Ring means that we are constantly guarding the dwelling. Its purpose is to allow us to be continually aware of the integrity of our dwelling. But this too means that we are continually aware that it is under threat. Our focus is now on our need to protect the dwelling rather than on it protecting us. The dwelling, thus, becomes a burden, an expensive asset that might turn into a liability. It is a cause for anxiety, another of the cares of the world instead of a place of caring for. We worry that something might happen to it instead of it keeping us safe. We remain on guard. We now see a greater threat of intrusion precisely because we have taken steps against it.

What about control inside dwelling? Echo aims to make our domestic lives more convenient. But we might question whether we are becoming more dependent on technology and so less able to use and control the dwelling ourselves. With these devices, there is an extra layer of mediation between us and the dwelling. Using Echo – asking Alexa – might make us less capable. It will certainly increase our sense of complacency, but it might also be heightening the sense of illusion that can take over our complacency. We feel safe, we feel more comfortable, but pre-programmed devices are acting – making decisions – for us on the basis of algorithms and common assumptions made external to the dwelling and based on generalised presumptions of behaviour.

In its advertising, Echo is shown doing tasks that are basically inconsequential, such as playing a particular piece of music or turning lights down. They can certainly do more than this and, as the technology develops, they will doubtless do so, connecting up to many other areas of our lives, such as banking and bill paying. In a few years, this might become the norm and we should, therefore, ask if this is something to be welcomed or, indeed, if it matters to any great degree. Should we not welcome it and see it as progress? What makes our lives easier must be a good thing, but we also need to remember that what these devices are replacing are the perfectly straightforward arrangements that we have already. We have no great difficulty in turning on a light or putting on some music, and there are already perfectly convenient and accessible means of paying our bills.

What may alter the situation though is when access through certain devices becomes the default. They might be taken up by government and the large companies and institutions we deal with, and in this situation, we would be forced to use them ourselves. There are many examples of this shifting of the default, such as the general insistence on paying salaries and wages into bank accounts in the 1980s through to paperless online billing in the 2010s. There is a presumption here that we wish to use the technology and are capable of using it. A majority may be able to become accustomed to this, even if some may cavil at the imposition of having to do so. But some households will struggle with it, for financial reasons or because of age and infirmity. There will also be knock-on consequences in terms of access to services. We are already seeing that one effect of online banking is mass branch closures causing difficulties for some people in accessing their accounts.

Technology forces us to remain up to date (on a timetable set by others) and alter our behaviour to fit into the new norm. It tends to do this under the banner of convenience and flexibility (even as it panders to our anxieties and insecurities). It will make our lives easier and we can then focus on more pleasurable things like playing with the children and shopping online. There does, indeed, tend to be a short period of flexibility where several options are offered. However, within a relatively short period, a new norm is imposed, and the older options are dropped as obsolete. It is certainly convenient to use online banking, and once we have become accustomed to it, there is no need to use any other method to pay bills and control our finances. But should we have a choice over whether we wish to manage our finances in this manner? If we lack the choice, then are we not becoming dependent on particular technologies? If they stop working, then so do we. Those with relatively recent laptops are now being encouraged to use cloud storage for their data. It is doubtless useful to be able to store and transfer large amounts of data and gain access to it when we choose, wherever we are, and via several devices. But the virtual 'warehouse' where our data are stored has to be reliable and permanently accessible, as does our connection to the Internet. If the cloud goes down, then we have no access to our data and no alternative means of retrieving it. The cloud is now the default, sold to us on the assumption that we do need to store lots of data but require quick access to it. The available software and hardware are now configured on this basis, and so the need for cloud storage becomes self-fulfilling. Of course, we can alter the default, but first, we have to understand what is happening. We are being offered a fixed path from which we can deviate only if we are sufficiently aware. We are presumed to want to go down this route: we are told that it is what we want, and most of us, most of the time, go along with it. We may not notice or care that we are being directed, but it is happening nonetheless.

So perhaps, the further we become dependent on technology, the greater the danger that complacency slips into illusion. We maintain the illusion of safety, control and convenience, but this now serves to mask our dependency on technologies that we cannot fully understand. Of course, because this is an illusion, we do not feel we are dependent. We feel that our lives have been made easier, and to an extent they have been. But this means an increasing distance from dwelling as something that we have made, and continue to make, ourselves.

A certain dependency on technology is not by any means new, however. Humans have always been dependent on some form of technology. A couple of weeks after the repair to our central heating pump we had a power cut. We spent all of 30 minutes without any power in the house whatsoever. It was 7.30 on a warm May morning, so there was no need for light or heat. However, power was cut for the whole neighbourhood taking out the local mobile phone masts as well. So, we had no TV, radio, Wi-Fi, phone signal, kettle or toaster, and the fridge and freezer were turned off. This is as near to isolation as we can get in the modern world, and it was a little discomforting. It occurred to me that, other than going out and trying to find someone to talk to – someone who would probably know no more than I did about what was going on – I had no means of finding out the cause or extent of the problem and whether it was a small or large issue. For all I knew, the nuclear winter was about to start.

This mild anxiety was partly due to my expectations about how connected I am to a range of devices. We tend to get used to what we have and we consider what are in reality add-ons and incidentals to our lives to be necessities. Prior to 1998, I had no TV, Wi-Fi or mobile phone. I relied on radio and my CD player (iTunes was still five years away). So, a power outage in 1998 would have caused less of a problem.

When discussing the idea of need with my students, I would always ask them the following question: *Imagine your house is on fire. You know all humans and pets are safely out. You can take one thing with you. What would it be?* I asked this question many times, the purpose being to bring out the difference between needs and wants and identify the concept of the imperative. Over many years of asking this question, more than half of the students said the same thing: they would reach for their mobile phones. A few mentioned their wallet or credit cards, and one person said she would take her wedding photo album. But the majority felt that they could not manage without their phones.[4] This led to interesting discussions about what we do need and why we feel we need things that are actually fulfilling wants and desires.

It is a cliché, and therefore true, that many people live through their phones, not because, properly speaking, they have to but because that is how we can all now live. What is properly incidental – the opposite of existential – now seems to be all-important to us. We have to stay connected, to be able to contact anyone immediately and to be contactable ourselves. We cannot miss a message or lose our contacts. We use our phones to find out about the world and store our memories. It is a torment to have to wait an hour, let alone a day, to be in touch with others. But many of us can remember a time when we had access only to public payphones and relied for information on only a few TV channels, newspapers (carrying news of yesterday's events) and the public library. Computers were the size of a house and outside of the experience of most of us. I do not see this as an idyllic time – in the 1970s, we also had to make do without central heating or double glazing. My point is one of expectations, and the opportunities and aspirations that create them. We had a different sense of what was normal for us to expect and so we acted accordingly.

During the half-hour power cut, I did not really need the technologies I usually have at my disposal. At 7.30 am, my main concern was not being able to boil a kettle to make a pot of tea. There was nothing I wanted to watch on TV, nothing I needed the Internet for and no one to ring at that hour. There was nothing that could not wait for an hour or two if need be. What troubled me though was the possibility of connection – or rather, the lack thereof. I felt isolated by not being able to connect even though I did not particularly need to. Of course, if I had slept for another hour as my wife did, I might not even have noticed any issue. But I was awake and all the clever devices around me were not.

What was being knocked here, as was the case when the heating pump went up in smoke, was my complacency. I could not use my dwelling as I would expect to. My normal routines of a leisurely breakfast while looking at the news online had been stymied and I was put out, albeit mildly and only for a few minutes. I could no longer take for granted my use of these devices. I had to notice how dependent I had become on them. We accept and accommodate what we are used to. When a new device comes along, we might see this as new and a real change, but we soon assimilate it into

---

4 Of course, the students always asked me what I would take. My choice was my notebook containing my current research, the contents being the only things that I could not hope to replace.

dwelling and take it for granted (for as long as it works). We may soon not notice what Ring, Echo or as yet uninvented devices do in our lives. But we will come to expect it.

The power cut lasted barely half an hour and then I got on with making my tea and reading the news on my laptop, any mild anxiety at being isolated from the world now gone. I set about my usual routines, assuming that things were working as they should, which, of course, they were.

My dwelling, like those of my neighbours, is full of technology, some very old and some recent. Some items we will keep for many years, while other things we will replace with newer versions or, if they become obsolete, with whatever made them obsolete. However, this is not the aspect of dwelling that I hold closest to me. It is not what seems to matter. I can admit that I depend on technology. But technology does not itself necessarily enhance dwelling. It may change its functionality and our ability to access it. Yet our use of dwelling remains distinct and is dependent on other things such as our relationships and the nature of care. Dwelling, after all, is something we do and not just something we have.

The boundary around us

We are always in place. We cannot, properly speaking, ever not be in place. We are always in some sense located. But there are distinctions to be made here. What gives a place its significance is that it is bounded. Dwelling is bounded by meaning. Its borders are where the specificity of meaning ends and this becomes just general space that could, we might say, be anywhere. There may be some meaning beyond the boundary, but it is of a distinctly different quality to that which is within.

The boundary of dwelling does not seem to be merely physical. We know that it can easily be breached. Its integrity depends on it being respected by others. We depend on their indifference, on their voluntary disregard for our place. We may be happy when some people cross our boundary, for example, to make a delivery. We may tolerate others, who are leafleting or canvassing. We may not relish the intrusion and may not be interested in what is being sold or canvassed, but we have no real objection to the person posting the leaflet or knocking on the door. We wish them no ill and do not believe they are acting improperly in coming to our door. If they did not come, we would not miss them, but this is not to say we would object or be offended.

We might ask then whether someone does have the right to put something through our letter box? Obviously, this depends on what is being put through: a leaflet is fine, but faeces or petrol and a lighted match are clearly not. It might be said that we encourage the intrusion – the leaflet if not the faeces – by having a letter box. We do not need to have one in our front door, even though it is part of UK culture to do so. We could, as is the case in some other countries, have a box at the perimeter of our property, or have a post office box to collect from on a regular basis. However, we choose to have the convenience of services that deliver to our door. Likewise, we will give ready access to some people such as meter readers from utility companies. We may have an external meter which can be accessed without our knowledge, but this is still on our property.

Returning to the subject of the broken central heating pump, we effectively handed parts of our house to the engineer for the duration of his visit. He entered the front door at will, turned taps on and off, drained our system and refilled it and went into several rooms and the loft to access tanks and pipes. He did not come into our living room, where he had no reason to be, but he moved around freely elsewhere. He played with the timer to the central heating and the thermostat, and I was more than happy to allow him to do so, all on the assumption that he knew what he was doing and was doing it competently and responsibly. He gave the impression of being both competent and fastidious, and the system has worked perfectly since his visit, so it proved to be quite proper to trust him. But all I had from this stranger was his credentials and my expectation of a person coming with those credentials. There was some mild anxiety before his visit (would he come? Was it readily fixable? etc.) and some relief when he left and the system seemed to be working properly.

The interesting point here is that I really wanted this stranger to have full access and take over my house, whereas in other circumstances, I would absolutely forbid it. As I told him, I was happy to 'leave him to it' while I tried to get on with other things. We needed this stranger's expertise to ensure that we could again take our place for granted and use it as we wished to. It was not functioning as it should, as we expected it to, and this made our normal life impossible. We would, therefore, happily forego some privacy for a short period of time to regain the full functionality of our dwelling again.

This was, of course, a relatively minor and straightforward issue, and there are times when a much more significant and lengthy intervention is required which might prevent us from using parts or even all of the dwelling. There may be times when the dwelling is in total upheaval, with some rooms unusable for a period and others taken up with storage. There may come a time part way through this process when we start to have doubts and regret ever beginning the change, especially if it is an improvement rather than an essential repair. Or perhaps, knowing the extent of the upheaval, we might delay making certain changes and improvements. Accordingly, we may be prepared to put up with the inconvenience of a sub-optimal dwelling for quite some time in order to put off a much greater inconvenience but over a much shorter period. We might tolerate noisy or inefficient machines and materials rather than replace them. In some cases, there may be a slow deterioration such that we hardly notice the decline in functionality, and so we grow used to it and bend with it. This is not a crisis, the dwelling can still be used well and we are not too inconvenienced. Things can be sustained as they are and have not yet gone far enough to need any intervention.

We may put off improvements partly or entirely for financial reasons: we do not have the money and need to save up. In this case, we have no choice. But it is not always a matter of money. It might be because we have other priorities – holidays are more important than new carpets – or we have very busy lives. Or it might be that we have a high tolerance level and are able to ignore cracks, abrasions, clunks and bangs, etc. Perhaps we are lazy and untidy, and so what would be intolerable for others is not a problem for us. Or we might have a disability or impairment which makes it impossible for us to do the improvements even though we would dearly wish to do so.

This situation applies even though, in many cases, we would not be doing to work ourselves. We are not competent to lay a stair carpet, or precision-cut a worktop or weld pipes. We would expect to get someone in who is competent and pay them. But we might still not have the work done, even though we have the money.

It might be that the property still functions well enough, and so, we feel that the work is as yet unnecessary. We may consider that what needs doing is purely aesthetic. The problem might be in a part of the dwelling that others do not see or which we do not use much other than to work in. It might not be damaging anything else. We might not entertain guests and so who else would see? We might have a lot going on in our lives, or some other issue or emergency that makes what would, otherwise, be a priority into something of little consequence. We may simply have more important things to worry about than the state of our dwelling. Some people, of course, may be unaware of the nature and extent of the problem. The seriousness of some issues only becomes apparent after a certain point, and then the repair might be very extensive and expensive, for example, with subsidence. But we have to be aware that people will have different tolerance levels, and this needs to be factored in with any aesthetic and financial considerations. This level of tolerance will even differ within households (teenagers might be more tolerant of untidiness than their parents).

But I would suggest we may delay mainly because we can still use the dwelling pretty much as we choose to. Its functionality is not really impaired at all, and so we feel we can put up with what we see to be only a minor problem. We perhaps know that we ought to get it resolved, but it does not seem to be a priority. It does not affect us, so why do we need to act today or tomorrow? Indeed, it might not be the only thing we are neglecting or delaying, and so, we plan to make the improvements: we are, we tell ourselves, definitely going to do them. But there is always something more pressing, more urgent that takes our attention and our resources. So, we put off the problem, and there are often not really any consequences in doing so (assuming we do not put things off for ever).[5]

All this relates to how we view our dwelling. Do we see it as an asset, with a tradable value that may allow us to move up the property ladder? Are we concerned with status and what the neighbours might think about us (or what we think they might think about us)? Is the dwelling a place that allows us to focus on other things such as relationships or work, or relaxing, reading, writing, gaming or whatever? Do we see it as a place of refuge rather than a place of display or as a quantifiable asset?

We use the dwelling. It is functional, a tool. But we also appreciate or deprecate it separately. We can see the things that need to be done, the repairs, cracks, repainting, etc. We may feel that there are 101 things that could be done, and we feel at times that the dwelling could be much more convenient. It does frustrate us that we are living like this. Yet it is still our home, the place in which we can relax, throw off our concerns and be free from the cares of the world. It is the very place where we do not have to do anything unless we wish to, where things do not matter. It is where we can safely, and without fear of sanction, put things off. We can be ourselves and we do not have to concern ourselves with what others might think or want us to do. We do not have to compare ourselves with anyone or anything else.

The lack of sanction, the fact that inaction is consequence-free, is so important here. It just does not matter if we do not do these things. They may be a small inconvenience and annoyance, but we have already put up with them and other issues for years. We are only accountable to ourselves and there is no one to tell us off but ourselves.

In this way, we tend to forget the complexity of the dwelling, thinking that it will work for us constantly. We believe this largely because the dwelling does work for us most of the time. Only a day or so after our central heating was repaired, the issue had receded into the background and we again just assumed that there would be hot water for a shower and that the heating would come on as required. Nothing had happened to alter that comfortable perception and we did not expect anything to come along to disabuse us. So, we could get on with our lives, certain of the continued

5 I am, of course, aware that there are some people who will not allow any minor fault to rest. They are, I would suggest, the exception rather than the norm.

amenity of the dwelling. In time, there will doubtless be further problems and we may decide to get on with all those little jobs that we have put off, and then the structure of the dwelling will move again into the foreground. But not for the moment.

Too much noise

In the 1980s, working as a housing officer, I tried to resolve a neighbour dispute between two elderly tenants. This was itself quite unusual as most disputes involved clashes between different types of tenants, most commonly when young and old were in too close proximity. In this case, the elderly couple in the ground-floor flat had complained that the similarly elderly couple in the flat above them were excessively noisy, stomping around at all hours. They particularly mentioned the regular and noisy flushing of the toilet, which they found intolerable. Their lives, they said, were being made a misery by the tenants above. In talking to the first-floor tenants, it soon become clear that the husband was quite ill and suffered from a serious bladder complaint necessitating regular trips to the toilet at all hours of the day and night. The tenants below were aware of this but did not see this as sufficient mitigation. The association carried out tests on the flush to see if the noise was excessive – it was not – and checked the flooring of the flat above to see if that might be a problem – again, it was not. The association concluded that the first-floor tenants were acting entirely reasonably according to their circumstances and that the ground-floor tenants were just being overly sensitive to noise. However, the latter would not accept this and persisted with their complaints. They simply had no sympathy for the plight of their neighbours and could see the situation only from their perspective. The dispute was only resolved when the first-floor tenants were forced to move because of the husband's illness.

Of course, there may have been some other motive at play here. There may have been an earlier falling out that no one involved was prepared to mention. However, this example does show the importance of tolerance. We have to be prepared to exclude ourselves and become indifferent to others. The indifference is not solely through not having to register the existence of those around us, although we may be able to do this, but also because we choose to exclude them.

We tolerate the behaviour of those we love and care for and make allowances for them that we might not do for others. Our care for those we love is active and intentional. However, we tolerate those we do not know in a rather different way, by remaining unaware of their situation and not involving ourselves in their lives. There is no intent on our part because we have no active engagement with them. What allows us to do this is the boundary that dwelling provides which excludes others. How others choose to live need not affect us because our mutual exclusion means we know nothing of each other. We only know how others live if they show and tell. We are quite free to avoid others. They need not impinge upon us, and this involves no active planning on our part. Most of the time, we do not even have to think about leaving others alone. We do not have to actively restrain ourselves because we live quietly within our own boundaries as they live quietly within theirs. We do not make ourselves noticeable.

But, of course, there are times when we do impinge, and we are not invisible. Others can be affected by our actions. But this will tend to remain comfortably within a tolerable level, and others are doing nothing that we ourselves do not do, whether it be chatting in the garden, mowing the lawn or having a barbeque. These impingements on our dwelling are at a very low level and are only temporary. We might wish that our neighbours were not having a barbeque, but we can also accept that they are doing nothing out of the ordinary and they are certainly not trying to offend. We are, therefore, prepared to accept actions that are themselves normal and reasonable. We tend to know what reasonable behaviour is by experience, and we ourselves refrain from behaviour which we feel falls outside of this norm. This is a form of care, even if it does tend to operate, as it were, through exclusion. We show our care by accepting the behaviour of others and so excluding them from our lives. This does not merely depend on our actions – we have to be reasonable with regard to the circumstances in which others find themselves – but without our acceptance of others, neither they nor we can live peacefully.

Who cares?

Who cares about how other people live? Why should we bother to consider this? What does it matter, we might ask, how anyone else treats their dwelling? There are, we might argue, many more important things for us to focus on, related to dwelling (as either a noun or a verb) or more generally. Should we not be focused on homelessness or affordability or security of tenure? Should we not be caring about the things that matter?

I can only acknowledge the relative importance of these issues, but that this is precisely the point. This is not because the issues of minor repairs and improvements are themselves negligible but because the very notion of 'who cares?' is at the centre of the issue. Those outside the dwelling do not have to care and, particular circumstances notwithstanding, perhaps they should not care. It is precisely who cares, who does not need to and who should not, that is important here.

The significance of dwelling is that it is a place that only some and not others should have to care about. The care should be very specific. Others, with no interest in that dwelling, should be indifferent and let the users do as they will. It would be an unwelcome and unbidden imposition for someone to interfere unless, of course, they were asked to. We do not expect others to comment on our dwelling and how we keep it. They can at best reserve their comments until they are out of our hearing.

Clearly, we will intervene if we feel something is unsafe or if we feel the person cannot cope. My wife and her sister have had to intervene ever more directly in the affairs of their elderly mother, eventually to the extent of persuading her to move into residential care. But throughout this process, they were careful to get their mother's permission for any action and present the situation as a choice she was making herself.[6]

There are many more important issues than wall cracks and noisy water pipes, and these issues should be the proper focus of our attention. But we do have the ability, opportunity and resources to deal with a range of issues, some of which may be some considerable way down the hierarchy of needs. What matters is the manner in which we address these problems. Whose resources do we use and whose time and skills do we take up? How do we allocate resources down the hierarchy of needs and who does that allocation, and at what point in the scale does the nature of the decision-making change? In particular, we need to determine what is properly private and personal and within the competence of individuals to use their own resources. What is solely the concern of the user and what has a wider public or societal impact? In other words, the question we need to answer is precisely 'who cares?' Just who should be doing what? This is about the allocation of priority and understanding risk, and appreciating which is a public and which a private issue. It is a matter of appreciating how the public and private might mesh together, and so where the grey areas might be. What we are looking at then is a matter of jurisdiction, and so the busy activist or policymaker, keen to prioritise and make a difference, is quite right to ask, 'who cares?'

---

6 As an aside here, but a crucially important one, the actions taken by my wife and her sister were entirely geared to keeping their mother in her own home, even to the point of both of them moving in and caring for her on a full-time basis. Only once their mother's health had deteriorated so far did they take the step of persuading her to move into residential care.

I do not want just anyone to care about my dwelling. It pleases me that most people are indifferent to it and me and focus instead on themselves (or I presume they do – I too am indifferent and so I am not looking at what they are doing). I want to limit those who care and who I care for. I want to restrict it to those who have an interest in me and my dwelling. There will be a hierarchy of interest here, with different people having more or less 'invested' in caring for me. I hope that my wife, my daughters, my sister and my former work colleagues all have some interest in my well-being. I hope they would all wish me well and want me to flourish. But I would expect rather different levels of interest from these people. I now hardly ever see my work colleagues and do not expect to. I see my sister several times a year and we enjoy each other's company and then go back to our respective families. I live with my wife and youngest daughter, and so we share many things together (although what I share with my wife is different from what I share with my daughter). My wife will inherit on my death and my daughters after that. I hope it is not a surprise to my former work colleagues that they will not.

In dwelling, no one can hear us. This might be a problem for us. But there are times when we wish to go unheard. We do not want others to hear us, and we do not want to hear from them. We only want certain people to hear us because of what we wish to say and because of who they are. What we wish to say is for them alone. There are certain things we will say – and do – when we are sure no one else can hear. We speak to people close to us in ways we would not to others, using words that are specific to our relationship with them (King, 2017b). We can only achieve this through the indifference of others.

We do not tend to notice or even acknowledge the indifference we have towards others. We are busy doing other things which matter to us more. We may not like to think of ourselves as indifferent, feeling it to be rather too negative. But this does not change the manner in which we do ignore others, even if we dislike the term being applied to us. Indeed, if we think about it, we know we are doing the right thing and are pleased that others are indifferent to what we wish to do in our dwelling. Indifference is not a conscious act, and this is why it is both constructive and benign.

Indifference means that people remain other, but they are not alien. We do not dislike those we are indifferent to. It is hard to be indifferent to those we dislike. Rather we are being benign in offering them their space. To keep our distance is to show care. There is no antagonism. It may be unthinking, in the sense that we are not really considering others at all, but why should we and why would we expect others to consider us? We are not specifically important to them and they are not specifically important to us. We do not wish to use them and do not think they are using us. We are focusing on what we should, on what we consider important. There is no obvious detriment in this and, indeed, some considerable benefit. We focus solely on those with an interest in us and allow others to do the same with those who matter to them.

I do not, properly speaking, care for those who live in the dwellings I can see from my study window. I wish these people, most of whom who I am on speaking terms with, no harm, and I hope they thrive and meet their aspirations. But I can and will do nothing actively to become involved with them. The best I can do is to ignore them and so put no obstacles in their path. I do nothing positive to help them and it would appear eccentric or perhaps even something more sinister if I were to try. There is nothing to stop me putting money anonymously through their letter boxes and I am sure they would spend it. If they saw me doing it, however, they might call the police.

My neighbour whom I only see to speak to once or twice a month, told me recently that his father, who must be quite elderly, is suffering from cancer. I responded to this as one does, with sympathy and allowed him to tell the story at his own pace and in his own way, offering support to him as he did so. As we parted, I wished his father all the best and reiterated my sympathy. There was undoubtedly a bit of ritual in this. My neighbour was telling me a story he has probably already told many times and I was reacting as I thought I should. Neither of us was being disingenuous: this is just how things are between people who know each other only slightly and who have little in common other than a shared border. I have seen my neighbour a few times since this conversation and I have always asked after his father's health, always, it must be said, with a degree of trepidation about what the answer might be, and the distress and embarrassment that might arise as a result.

This is, I think, the appropriate limit of my interest. There is, of course, a lot more I could do, but not much of it would be appreciated. For instance, if I were to knock on my neighbour's door and ask specifically after his father's health, it might be seen as a little odd. If I suggested that next time my neighbour visits his father (who I have never met and know nothing about other than his health condition) I might go along too, I'm sure this would be taken badly. It might be seen as a joke in poor taste. It would certainly be seen as very strange behaviour. It is, of course, something I would never dream of doing. I can show an interest in my neighbour's father's health, but only up to a certain well-established limit that recognises my neighbour's autonomy and privacy. I am not part of his life, he does not appear to wish me to be and we have little in common with each other. We do all the usual neighbourly things – taking in parcels or borrowing tools, but this is common neighbourliness. This is indifference as it actually is, where we know that there are limits which we must respect for our own and the others' benefit. There is nothing callous or calculating about this, but this is just how we behave with others who have others to care for them. We do what is appropriate and only that, and this involves retaining a certain distance. In any society, there are appropriate ways to behave, and how we dwell helps configure and is configured by those ways. They will be largely unspoken, seldom articulated and infrequently broken. We will usually accept these norms of behaviour without question. These are the limits that make dwelling possible for all of us at the same time, and this applies regardless of what rules apply in any one place at any one time. They allow us to live as we expect to live.

The fact that strangers do not care is as important to me as the fact that those close to me do care. It is the indifference of strangers that makes my life liveable in the manner I wish it to be. I depend on their quite natural desire to discriminate between those close to them and myself as a stranger.

I do not take this indifference to be in any way callous. If I saw a neighbour in trouble, I would help them without question. I do not wish to ignore the plight of others, and I am not suggesting that we should only focus on ourselves. This form of indifference says nothing about our propensity to give to charity or our general responsibility for our fellow citizens. *But it says everything about how we should express it.* We show care when we can and do this by giving to charity or by volunteering or helping out a neighbour who we know needs it. But what we do refrain from doing is interfering in the legitimate autonomous actions of individuals. If they are in control of their affairs, then we should leave them to it. If they do not ask for help, we should not force it on them. Rather we do as they expect and leave them alone so that they can do as they wish, just as we expect to be left free to pursue our own ends. Our indifference is mutual and benign. There is nothing that we are neglecting here.

To interfere where this is not wanted would not be benign and might be damaging, and this would apply even in cases where we thought we might know better. Whether we do think we know better, and consider ourselves more intelligent, practical or moral, does not really matter. We have no right to interfere, and we cannot expect to have our autonomy respected if we do not respect that of others. In this sense, indifference is more than benign but is a matter of mutuality that makes a civilised life possible.

It may appear strange to see indifference as benign, but this is clearly the case where we depend on mutual exclusion from each other's affairs. What matters here is that we recognise and appreciate where the proper limits are: where does benign indifference end and neglect take over? We need to care for those who cannot look after themselves and have no one else.

We need some means of becoming aware of those in need. What we must avoid, however, is any drift to a more generalised interference on the basis that we are only 'doing good'.

What will tend to prevent this drift is our natural tendency to look inwards. It really is not very hard for us to ignore others. We have a natural regard for those to who we are related to and have commitments. This regard is more properly stated as *love*. We have absolute and rigid commitments to specific others for whom we are prepared to sacrifice ourselves. Care is the expression of love. It is the normalisation, the habituation, of sacrifice (King, 2017a).

Love is where my sacrifice helps and improves me as well as my loved ones. It makes me a better person because I show care to that specific other. This though is a by-product. We do not love another to benefit ourselves. We love them for themselves and as themselves. But in doing this, we are strengthened and we benefit.

The exception to this is where the love is not fully or sufficiently reciprocated, where the relationship is not mutual and so one person is constantly being drained by the other (King, 2017b). This though can happen, so to speak, voluntarily. One person can show love to someone who does nothing comparable in return. That, though, may not be the fault of the latter who may tell their lover that their love is neither wanted nor reciprocated, but this may be ignored, and the lover carries on. This is a waste of time and may end up being harmful to both parties if the love becomes obsessive.

Neither love and care can be quantified nor should they be. They cannot be accurately measured. What I mean by 'I love you' may differ from what the person to whom I say it might infer or mean if she were to say it herself. There is no way to measure this. In most cases, we might love each other 'enough' (defined in the sense that we never have to define it) for it not to matter.

Likewise, when someone says, 'You don't care', they do not necessarily mean it absolutely. It often really means that the other does not care enough or consistently or in the way expected or appreciated by the speaker. I can feel that I care enough and do all I can (or am prepared to do), but this might appear inadequate or inappropriate to whom I am supposed to be caring for. I may insist that I care deeply – and this may be true, in the sense that I sincerely believe that I do care deeply – but it does not appear so to the other. We can ask whose fault is this. Is it mine for failing to meet the expectation of the other, or theirs for having unreasonable and unrealistic expectations? Is it the fault of the carer or the cared-for?

The issue of vulnerability is relevant here, in that a relationship is not likely to be equal or symmetrical in its reciprocity (King, 2017b). One will be giving much more than the other. So we might want to concentrate on the care needs of the vulnerable. But whereas this might be clear in a professional relationship – nurse to patient, for example – it is much less so in a personal relationship. In a private relationship, there may be asymmetry, but no formal means of redressing it (no policies, regulations, professional ethics, etc.), and so it is very much down to the individuals involved in that particular relationship.

It may be the case though that it is not clear or consistent who carer and cared-for are. Things may change over time or as circumstances alter (a busy period at work, illness, anxiety and stress). The balance in a relationship may shift over time. In many relationships, care is mutual and is not obviously asymmetrical. At different times, and with different issues, there will be shifts in the balance, but the relationship will still be about mutual support. Care can then be largely unthinking, and it need not be consciously applied. Care takes the form of habits and tacit forms of behaviour which are routinised and not explicit.

Care is not for show. It is not a matter of showing that one cares, but of caring without show. Caring is only demonstrated by and through the regularity of our actions. There will be times when it is more explicit or overt (anniversaries and special occasions, illness, reminiscing over defining memories, etc.), but these themselves are natural and come from within the relationship. Mostly, care takes place simply through our being there, being reliable and trustworthy, following routines and acting as expected. In this way, the care does not appear special; it is not premeditated and needs no specific trigger. It is always there as part of the relationship. Indeed, care cannot be differentiated from the routines and habits of the relationship.

In long-standing relationships, there may be no overt or public shows of affection. Being together is enough. There is no need for any demonstration or publicity. These relationships are at the stage where care can be relied on and there is no need to test it. The care is so ingrained into habits and routines it does not appear as a separate entity.

Indeed, we might argue, as does Erich Fromm (1995), that to say frequently, 'I love you' to someone is a sign of insecurity, of a weak love. A strong love need not speak out; it does not need telling. This sounds superficially convincing, and in some relationships, it may be the case that couples find no need to say these words to each other.

To say, 'I love you' to someone is comforting to both – to the one who hears it and the one who feels able to say it. It may be that the reason one says it is to get a reciprocal response. The declaration might then be seen as 'needy', as a sign of dependence on the other. Yet what is a loving relationship if not one where each party *needs* the other and is, in some way, dependent on the other? We might also consider what type of love would create and reinforce independence and autonomy? One is not in a relationship, we must suppose, to be separate or to exploit that person. The relationship exists presumably because of an attraction and a commitment that may be reinforced by formal vows, which, according to all major religious traditions, are taken to be sacred. There is an absoluteness coming out of these sacred vows and to say, 'I love you' is to reinforce that and to remind each other of that sacred state. It would be a much greater problem were one not able to say those words, perhaps out of fear that the feeling would not be reciprocated.

We might say the words, 'I love you' because we already know how each of us feels about the other. We do not depend on the response, but it does us good to say the words and hear the response. There is some 'neediness' in this, if by this we mean that we need the other person, have grown reliant on them and want to be with them. Saying 'I love you' gives a context and a purpose to care. It is why we care and so it becomes, so to speak, the non-routinised way of demonstrating it.

Dwelling is where sacrifice becomes care. The sacrifices we make in order to care for those we love extend rather than diminish us. Dwelling is where we make, maintain and strengthen our bonds and where duty is joy, a fulfilling act. We do things because we love, to show love and because we are loved. This is implicit in our every action. But we can only achieve this by the exclusion enabled by dwell which, in turn, gives meaning to inclusion.

Dwelling allows us to select who we wish to include and exclude. There is undoubtedly the potential for cruelty in this, but this is as nothing compared to the cruelty of never being able to select and to be prey to all, of being forced to include all who may come near and exclude no one other than by successive acts of force. This is the fate of those without dwelling. The most powerful definition of homelessness is the inability to exclude unwanted others from our lives. This definition contains all the threat, all the nakedness and emotionally crippling vulnerability, all the violence and all the abuse inherent in homelessness. And more generally, it shows the significance of dwelling as enclosure, where it is possible to be loved and where there are those particular ones who care.

We all share

There is conflict in dwelling. There is limited space for any of us and we may only have a limited ability to escape. There may have to be restrictions on our freedom and use of space so that we can accommodate others. Our use of dwelling might be competitive, and this means there will be a need for negotiation between ourselves and those we share with. We may not always get on with those we share with. Our interests may clash and there will be misunderstandings. We may grow tired of those close to us and weary of the effects of our prolonged proximity. But all of this is within the context of our connectedness with those we are close to. Indeed, these may be the very deepest of connections, of marriage, partnership and family ties. The depths of these connections may mean that we cannot leave easily. We may be financially or materially dependent. We may be too young or too old and not competent to look after ourselves. But it may also be that the convenience of our situation outweighs the occasional issues we might have with those we share with. Or we may just lack options.

Dwelling excludes outsiders and includes loved ones. But within the inclusion, it can be very difficult, if not impossible, to exclude. We are committed to sharing our lives with those we have included, but at times they intrude upon us, when we are tired, ill, in a mood after a hard day at work or whatever, and we find them tiresome and incapable of understanding us. We might feel that we cannot get sufficient distance from them, but in these circumstances, the last thing we wish to do is to leave the dwelling.

Dwelling is made more difficult by other people. They wish to use the space too and apparently believe that they have the right to do so as much as we have. We have to understand and get used to this, but it is not always easy for us to do so. There is only so much that we hold in common, and we can never fully – or perhaps even partially – know what another is really thinking and feeling. We can never be absolutely sure that their statements truly reflect their private thoughts and feelings. In any case, we are prone to misunderstand or misinterpret the statements and actions of others, based on our preconceptions. No matter how close we are, we remain separate in important and necessary ways.

We may not even be sure that we agree on what it means to share. Does sharing mean concurrent or serial use? Sharing depends on space and the use of space. Can we use a particular space together, or only in turn? Some things cannot be used by more than one person at the same time.

Does sharing mean equality of use? What are the restrictions and limitations on use in particular situations or times? What are the power and authority relations involved? Does our propensity to sacrifice and forego things for the other have to be equal and reciprocated? Indeed, does sharing mean the same as reciprocating? Parents do not share equally with children and it would be absurd to expect it, as well as impractical. Parents give far more than their children and do so without conditions or the need for reciprocity. Parents might still help their children when they are adults, still allowing them to live free at home and without paying for much. This seems entirely natural to me. My dwelling is also my daughters' dwelling, even if they spend little time there. When they come, they can and do use the dwelling as if it is theirs and always has been. It helps that finance is not an issue for us, but in most cases, parents would make sacrifices rather than deny their children full support.

Not all things in dwelling may be held in common. We may see certain things as being truly *mine* and beyond sharing. We might also ask how far the past impacts here. Would a past misunderstanding – where we inadvertently forgot to share something that we were expected to – impact on our next engagement with that person? And can we agree on the things that we never share, or will this be a source of conflict?

Do we still keep secrets and so unilaterally refuse to share certain things? Is it always wrong for us to do so? Does this depend on the nature of the secret, or whether both parties keep secrets (assuming we can both know this)? Is mutual secret keeping better or worse than only one doing this, or, in other words, is it better to know the other keeps secrets or not? Do we keep the same sorts of things secret and are they of the same scale and import? How much does timing matter here as well as the gravity of the issue? At what point does keeping a secret become a betrayal? Can it ever be legitimate to keep a secret? If one has no inkling of the other's secret, then is it a problem? Does it only become a problem once we know? Is one living a lie before anyone knows about it? Would it be better not to know and retain our peace of mind? How could we possibly know, and it remain a secret?

To cut through all these questions, we might ask another one: why should sharing mean the same to everyone? We might agree on a very general and non-specific definition of the word, but once it comes to the specifics of a relationship, of real shared use and the different attitudes we might have, then there can be problems. We will have different tolerance levels, and we might not always be equally accepting of things. We have different affinities, and our connections to things and others need not be the same. Relationships can be, and often are, asymmetrical. We will have different emotional responses to things and do not necessarily share the same interests and obsessions. But we can still share.

At the ends of life

Our children are our responsibility and this is not something that be passed on to anyone else, and the same applies to our elderly parents. Whatever the role of the state, and how state services might be funded, we are still, in most cases, to be there as the primary carers. The default is family care within dwelling.

There may be clashes and conflicts in dwelling, but in most situations, there are clear priorities. Very young children cannot do many things for themselves, and their parents, therefore, step in and act without question. As children get older and more proficient, these interventions diminish, becoming ever more inappropriate and unnecessary. Indeed, it is this tapering of intervention that causes most of the clashes and conflicts, which are often disputes about what is appropriate and necessary.

At the other end of life, there comes a time when elderly parents struggle to live independently, something often exacerbated by the loss of their life's partner. Their children will often need to step in here and offer increasing levels of support and care, often to the extent that they will be living with their parents again. This may involve returning to the parental home – not always literally, of course – after a period of maybe 40 years or more, and intervening to provide care in the opposite direction from when they were living with their parents.

The care that children offer to their parents in this situation is as unconditional as that once provided by their parents, but there is a fundamental difference, in that the interventions often involve the (entirely necessary) infringement of the parent's dignity. The parent may need help with private activities such as bathing and using the toilet that they have been quite able to undertake on their own. This is more than a simple reversal of the parent/child relationship. While the child now becomes the primary carer, the parent is reduced to having the capabilities of a young child. But this often meshes with the resurfacing of old habits and relationships within the parental home. The dynamic here is quite different as the dependencies have been reversed even as the old relations are still quite well understood by both parties.

It is, moreover, a situation that is unlikely to last. It is not a permanent situation, no matter how far the habits of the past seem to be reintroducing themselves. On the one hand, the children can only put their lives on hold for a limited time, especially if they have work and family commitments. But, on the other hand, the parent's capabilities will continue to decline. There will then be something of a competition of priorities between the parental and family dwellings. Priorities may remain clear, but there will still be some pulling in different directions. What mitigates this competition between priorities is the declining capabilities of the elderly parents. As the decline advances the priorities may become all the clearer, but added to this is the understanding, often left unsaid, that this decline means the situation will not be a permanent and stable one.

The care of children leads to their development and a situation where they become ever more independent and capable of acting for themselves. But caring for a parent is one of mitigating a declining situation.

The parent's capabilities will continue to decline and the level of care needed will only increase and perhaps eventually get to a stage where care can only be provided by professionals outside of the family. The elderly parent will become less able to deal with the implacability of dwelling and find it increasingly difficult to negotiate through the space. It may be possible to make adaptations, but these will only be temporary as faculties decline further. While young children learn to manage stairs, use the toilet and wash themselves, the elderly, as it were, unlearn and need ever greater levels of assistance. This means that habits become increasingly unstable and new regimes need to be created to protect the person and mitigate their declining capabilities. These too will always be temporary and will inevitably be compromised by crises and continual decline. The result of this is unpredictability, which is the very opposite of what dwelling exists to maintain.

In general, parents know what to expect as a child develops. There are a number of stages, which may happen at different times for each child but, in normal conditions, will certainly be gone through. This does not happen with the elderly. Their mental and physical capacities will decline, but not in any predictable or prescribed order nor over any particular time period. Decline may be precipitated by crises such as illness or accidents. There is no steady pattern as there is with child development. It is then impossible for the normal complacency of dwelling to embed itself and for habits to become grooved, in any proper sense.

One means by which children develop is through the effective management of boundaries and exclusion within the dwelling. Children increasingly engage in activities without their parents and in time become used to having their own private space. The more they develop, the more privacy they expect and the more is granted. But this works the other way with the elderly, and their effective capacity to safely exclude others lessens. It becomes dangerously inappropriate to allow the same level of privacy that even a pre-teen child might expect.

Much of the situation is managed reluctantly by the family carers. The elderly person may resent their lack of independence and still recall their more functional relationship with their children. This might mean that certain rituals must be enacted to preserve the dignity of the person and at least some semblance of independence even though the grown-up children are now doing precisely what their parents once did for them: feeding, washing and so on. Yet the children remember their parents as they were, and so instead of the promise of development, there is the shadow of further decline hanging over the relationship.

Cares of the world

We should consider the cares of the world as distinct from care in dwelling. The cares of the world have no end. They are boundless, limitless and beyond measure. Care in dwelling is bounded. It may involve us in considerable effort, but it is within distinct limits. It is also only known to those who are party to the dwelling and, therefore, those within its limits. This care does not, or should not, go beyond the boundary and not be widely shared. We do not want this care to be shared.

The cares of the world are negative. It is 'care' seen as problems, anxieties and burdens. It is not love or 'looking after' and being with and for others. Cares of the world are burdens under which we struggle. Care in dwelling is where we are besides others, alongside them. We are part of them and they are part of us. They are with us and not against us. We might be caring for a loved one, in the sense that they need a lot of attention. This is, we might say, a chosen situation and so is a different sort of burden, if it is even considered a burden at all. We have taken up this care, whether out of duty or willingly, rather than having it thrown at us. In dwelling, care is something we take up. Cares of the world, however, bear down on us. There is weight in both, but with distinctly different motives, and motive matters greatly here.

Dwelling helps us escape from the cares of the world. It offers a boundary, a barrier against ingress. Dwelling helps us evade the imposition of external responsibility and burden. We often feel relieved and can relax when we get home. We cast off the cares of the world and free ourselves. No longer have we external expectations to fulfil, no longer are we judged and held to account. We can limit our care to those people and things that matter to us. Without boundaries, we cannot exclude the cares of the world but are continually prey to their oppression. We need the means to exclude these cares, and this is the role taken by dwelling.

This does not mean dwelling is always benign. Exclusion can allow for abuse to hide, or cruelty to exist untrammelled. At times, we can face burdens that seem as nearly limitless as they can be, whether this is caring for the long-term sick, living in an abusive relationship or being dominated by another. These are very real and must not be dismissed. But neither should we see them as defining dwelling. These are the exceptions, which being so help us to see how dwelling really is. These are where the 'rules' are proven because they do not seem to apply. We should not write off the good because it is not the best.

The place of suffering

We cannot live without suffering. For some, such as Arthur Schopenhauer (1969) and Thomas Ligotti (2018), suffering is the very heart of life and there is nothing beyond it. Suffering is the only constant in life to the extent that we might even question why we have been born. After all, none of us asked to be put on this planet. Something of a less pessimistic view is provided by Jordan Peterson (2018), who argues that while suffering is a constant, we progress as human beings by fighting to overcome it. But whether we are deeply pessimistic or just see ourselves as realists, suffering is here and has to be faced for what it is.

In Ligotti's short stories, the main characters are always loners who cannot or will not connect with others (Ligotti, 2015). There is no such thing as society in Ligotti's bleak and dark worlds and no sense of care for others (or even for oneself). We either suffer or inflict suffering on others. Ligotti's worlds are without dwelling. There is no complacency, no taken-for-grantedness, only the uncanny and the macabre.

We might say that for Ligotti there is nothing that is *heimlich* or homelike. Yet the uncanny – the *unheimlich* – as Freud (2003) knew, depends on the homelike, on those experiencing the uncanny maintaining an expectation of the normal. There cannot then only be the uncanny, and this might lead us to suggest that there is also something beyond suffering. If there is suffering, and we are conscious of our suffering, then there must be a state of non-suffering.

I would suggest that the existence of the homelike is our surety against suffering. I do not suggest that we can live without suffering, but we can assuage it and there are remedies for it. One of these remedies can be found in dwelling. We live together in mutuality with others who can support and defend us. Being close to others means that we can see their suffering and respond to it: they are not alone in what they are going through. We form bonds of love and care, and through this inclusion, we can put up a barrier against suffering. It can isolate suffering, ensuring either that it cannot enter or that others are not infected or influenced by it.

Dwelling then can help us to find relief or avoid suffering, through the comfort and security it offers and the intimacy which it protects (Bachelard, 1969; King, 2004). Yet, we also need to consider that dwelling may not always be homelike and, thus, may itself be a site of suffering. It might be where we suffer from violence or abuse, hidden from public view and with no one to intervene. It might be where we suffer from the pain of loneliness and isolation. We may fear the loss of our dwelling, or we may feel that we suffer relative to others, in that our dwelling is not of a sufficient standard to meet our expectations and aspirations. Our dwelling may be a drain on us financially, physically and emotionally if it is too expensive, too large or impractical or because of who is no longer present with us. It may be of a poor quality, and so, we suffer from ill health or a sense of insecurity and impermanence. Most of all, we may suffer through a complete lack of dwelling. Perhaps we suffer most where we cannot exclude anyone or anything from our lives whether it be hostile strangers or the cold and rain.

But we need to make a distinction here between, on the one hand, suffering in dwelling regardless of the nature of dwelling and, on the other hand, suffering caused by dwelling, as a result of what it lacks or does or does not allow. This latter option can be further split into two: suffering caused by the general characteristics of dwelling such as privacy and exclusion and suffering caused by a particular dwelling which has a specific lack, such as being too small, overcrowded or damp. So, dwelling might be merely the incidental site of suffering, or suffering might result from the general qualities of dwelling, or to a specific issue in one particular dwelling relative to the needs of those using it. Clearly, the latter case can be dealt with more readily, through either repairing the dwelling or providing a better one. In the first case, where dwelling is incidental, we can perhaps suggest that there is little we can do as the issue does not pertain to dwelling. Instead, we should go directly after the cause of the suffering. The more intractable case is where suffering is due to characteristics inherent to dwelling. In this sense, we might have to conclude that suffering is inevitable and unavoidable, and we have to come to this reluctant conclusion for the simple reason that dwelling itself is unavoidable. We cannot live without dwelling and the care that comes from inclusion and exclusion. What we have to rely on is the belief, which we hope is reasonable and justified, that suffering is not all we have and all we are. Most of us, most of the time, do not suffer, and when we do, we know that our dwelling can help assuage the suffering.

In praise of banality

There is an exquisite banality to dwelling. It is just so ordinary, so normal, so full of those little things that are easy to mock and write off as unimportant, and – unforgivably – so bourgeois.

Dwelling is delightfully common. There are all those people doing the same things while believing they are individual and unique in their tastes and choices.

Dwelling is wonderfully inconsequential. Nothing we do matters all that much. There is nothing that could not be done differently or not done at a different time. None of the routines we insist on are really essential. The furniture need not be arranged as it is. We do not need to store our breakfast cereals in that one particular cupboard. We do not always have to sit in the same seat for dinner. These, we might say, are merely learned procedures developed without reason or true purpose and which we now imbue with a false significance. We just do things in a certain way, no matter how unreasonable and unthinking this is, and then insist on sticking rigidly to these ways. They become the *laws* of dwelling. And they simply do not matter. Dwelling then is where we use things without deliberation.

To us dwelling is both ordinary and exceptional (King, 2005). It is as it always is, and it must continue to be so if we are to live well. And we feel that we have made this one dwelling as it is. We believe we have moulded it to suit us. It defines us precisely because we have individually defined it. It is absolutely, specifically *ours*. We know it intimately.

Dwelling mixes the banal and the profound in intimate relation. We share breakfast and small talk with a person we have committed our lives to and who we tell our most intimate thoughts and feelings, share our anxieties and our hopes with, all amidst the chat about TV programmes, the state of the garden and the weather. The profundity of this is in the very fact that we need not see it as profound. We can proceed day to day, just like the weather: changeable but always there.

But just as we do this, we also know that our dwelling is made up of stock items, many of them similar if not identical to those of our neighbours, and all available through mainstream retail outlets. Dwellings and their contents are standardised and full of mass-produced items. Our dwelling is different only by being self-chosen, not because it is bespoke. The dwelling and its contents are all off-the-shelf. Its uniqueness depends on our continued – and continuous – sense of self and autonomy to dwell in something that is *ours and only ours*, even as we know we are doing this in common and in readily understandable ways (King, 2004, 2008).

Choice in dwelling is not an illusion. We really do choose. But we do so from a limited range of similar things. We all have tables and chairs, bathroom suites, kitchen units, shower fittings, beds and so on. Very few of us have these specially made. We may not be able to afford to have them made for us or see the need for it. We choose what is readily available and we will change things as fashions and technology change. Indeed, this technological change may alter the way we use the dwelling; for example, the use of portable devices can be said to a certain extent to individualise leisure and information gathering (Morley, 2000). So, it could be said that we are being led by our consumption of standardised products. Yet, despite this, we retain our belief in the uniqueness of our dwelling. It is the unique sum of non-unique parts. We might not create anything ourselves, but we have chosen what we have, and we choose to use things as we do, and so they *are* unique to us. We control them because they are ours and we can exclude others from them.

But there is more to consider here about choice in dwelling. Dwelling is, indeed, where most choices are without consequence. Yet, it is also where many of our most consequential steps are taken. We make regular choices such as what breakfast cereal to eat and what clothes to wear. But dwelling is also where we choose to start a family, or decide to change jobs or end a relationship. In the midst of the inconsequentiality – *because* of the inconsequentiality – we are able to take decisions of considerable consequence.

Returning to the issue of technology, we can say that it affects dwelling, but at its periphery rather than its core. It does not affect the notion of boundaries, care or exclusion. Technology can alter use in many ways, but it still requires our acceptance of it. We retain the ability to exclude technologies as immediately and as effectively as any other form of intrusion. Machines have 'off' switches. We really do not need to look at our laptop or phone. We may feel compelled to – technologies have an ability to create their own demand – yet this is still within the range of intentionality and choice. Technology does not really coerce us, even if we do feel a bit of a tug.

Certain technologies may be said to individualise or privatise activities, but much of the debate on this, as I argued in *Private Dwelling* (King, 2004), is predicated on a presumption towards the society which has never really held within dwelling. Dwelling is a private space that we use to exclude those who are not close to us. But we have to remember that many of the activities using these individualising technologies involve external communication and the sharing of a common experience. We may be on our own, but we are watching the same things as many, many others. We watch *Game of Thrones* and then talk to our friends about it on social media. So, technology may alter the manner in which we engage, but not necessarily what we engage with or whom.

Dwelling then is a shared banality, but this banality is fundamental to each of us and on our own terms. Dwelling, for all of us, is at the core of our being, but that core is expressed in a very ordinary manner. The very real complexity of dwelling can be reduced to the elemental ordinariness of our passage through it. This passage consists of the taken-for-granted use of self-chosen things, which may well not in themselves be unique to us.

Dwelling is fundamental and ordinary, essential and inconsequential, such that we forget its existentiality and concentrate instead on its by-product, the physical structures and the things we put in it. But these things are not the important part of dwelling. Rather it is its very lack of consequentiality that makes dwelling so significant. It is a place where it is quite safe for things not to matter. We only need to care for certain people and certain things and, perhaps for a time, we can care for nothing. Dwelling is where we can apparently be free of events.

This inconsequentiality can make it appear that we are focusing on the wrong things, and this is why policy thinking is dominated by the material and quantity, the by-products of dwelling. Yet, what really does matter is precisely that which appears not to, and it matters because it is in the background and not the foreground. It is so significant to us because it can go without notice and so appear inconsequential. It has to remain beyond speculation and stay implicit. To talk about dwelling is, so to speak, not to be using it.

Trying to say significant things about dwelling is foolish: it is trying too hard. The significance of dwelling is that we take it as insignificant, as unimportant, compared to what we choose to focus on. When we consider dwelling, we bring to the foreground what ought to remain in the shadows. We focus on the stage rather than the play, as if we should judge the performance based on the props and the scenery rather than the acting and the script.

It is perhaps natural to focus on what can be readily seen and what we can measure. This is why policy thinking tends to concern itself with quantity. But dwelling is about quality. It is about the meanings we attribute to things. But this presents those looking at dwelling with a problem: it becomes impossible to measure its value to us (Turner, 1976), particularly as the meanings are often implicit or unconscious. There is little that is deliberative and open about the meanings we attach to dwelling. They remain unstated, and this is because they do not have to be stated. No one else need take notice of them and we would hope that they would not. What is meaningful is quite properly behind closed doors, and we are too happily occupied behind our own closed door to give this any thought. We are quite naturally interested in our own lives, but not necessarily in those of others, and so we do not notice what they are doing. We know in very general terms how they live, but this is because of how we live. What we do not wish to know are the specifics behind those doors closed to us.

All of us who dwell know how dwelling is used and how deeply significant it is. But all that we know well – intimately, we might say – is our own, and we do not take this purely subjective experience as having any great significance beyond ourselves. We would perhaps not wish it to. Our dwelling is only significant to us, and we do not feel the need to share it. It would be of no interest to others. To broadcast our habits might come across as being in poor taste or as self-regarding. We might find it embarrassing to talk about ourselves in this way and so we refrain. We might talk about the value of our house. This might seem to be something we have in common in the sense we assume a shared interest in the quantitative aspects of dwelling. We might discuss television programmes about dwelling, interior design and house renovations, and again, these are quantitative. We might talk about problems and crises exterior to us such as the plight of the homeless we see in the streets or the tragedy of the Grenfell Tower fire. But we are much less likely to talk about how we ourselves use dwelling itself.

We do not expect dwelling to surprise us. This should never happen. We depend on its dull regularity. A surprise will mean that it has ceased to work as we expect it to. So we want our dwelling to be dull and regular. If we notice it, then something has gone wrong with it. Dwelling should be free of adventure. We need a place free of risk to plot and plan our journeys into a world full of adventure, risk and uncertainty. We need a safe place, a base, somewhere to which we can return. Dwelling is a place where we can recall, or dream of risk and adventure, where it is safe to play with our thoughts and desires. So we might say that it is, indeed, not banal to think that dwelling matters. But it matters that we know dwelling to be banal.

Complacency and the ordinary

Dwelling is where we have no need ever to justify how we behave. It is a place where we have licence. This is not unlimited, but it is considerable. We can be who or what we wish to be, even if we fail, and any failure will seldom have any serious consequences beyond our own conscience. Dwelling is the place where we are free to be stupid without having to justify this to anyone else. We can say and do things that we would not, and should not, do elsewhere.

Nothing about dwelling is hard apart from the walls we hide behind. It is this hardness that makes the rest as easy as it is. We do not even notice that it is easy. It is normal and just as it always is, and we just carry on without expecting anything other than what we have.

We can, of course, try quite hard within dwelling, but only because we do not have to. Dwelling is the safety net. Any failure is hidden, and we remain safe and protected. Dwelling is where our expectations can be safely held. Dwelling is acceptance, and so we should accept it as it is (King, 2008).

Acceptance is where we recognise the implacability – the hardness – of dwelling. We accept what it can and will do for us, and what it cannot and will not. There is a certain extent to which dwelling can be moulded. We can try to change it to suit ourselves. Dwelling will not react to us. It will remain, so to speak, passive. But there are limits to how far it can be moulded and keep its integrity. We can try to make up our own rules, but dwelling will not always listen.

Dwelling can and often will be shared, but it is not open. Access is always limited by some factor. Not everyone can be settled *here*. Dwelling involves the acceptance of limits. By limits we come to know ourselves and our place, but not merely by being circumscribed. Limits allow us to find ourselves properly, to set a pattern from which we can grow in our own way.

Dwelling is where we can be, and should be, complacent (King, 2014, 2017a). We are at peace with the world around us and see no reason to fight it or rage against it. We can just remain as we are in reasonable contentment. Complacency is where things are simply absorbed into our world. We are able to absorb elements from outside and incorporate them into our ordinary lives without necessarily feeling that we are changing. Complacency is where nothing seems to matter or has to matter. Things can and will just go on as we expect them to. We need not think about anything. There is no need for a purpose.

Complacency depends on our sense of the ordinary. The ordinary 'is what belongs to our customary world. It is what we would expect from the world around us' (King, 2005, p. 31). As Stanley Rosen (2002) has stated, 'Ordinary experience is what usually happens' (p. 267). If there is a rule that governs our experience, what we might term human nature, the ordinary is that which follows the correct application of that rule. An ordinary ac then is one that does not change the limits of the world (Gould, 2003). There are common rules and laws, which hold in most cases and most of the time (King, 2005).

According to Rosen (2002), the ordinary is defined by regularity, unity and comprehensiveness. It depends on the coherence of space time and the regularity of the natural order. The ordinary is what we are in the midst of. It is where we see the world as a unity that precedes us and which will continue after us. The world did not begin with us. It does not depend on our experience of it, and it is not formed by our experience. Our experiences are added to what is already a unity of experience. We seem to exist within a coherent continuity.

This sense of the ordinary can be linked to what I have called the three epistemological qualities of housing (King, 2003, 2005). These qualities are permanence, predictability and understandability, and an appreciation of these is crucial to any description of how we are able to control dwelling. Our need for housing is permanent; in that whatever our current circumstances are, we maintain the need for good quality housing. What differs for us is not the need for housing itself, but the current level of its fulfilment. This leads to the second quality of predictability, in that the permanence of our need for housing means that we are able to determine not only what we require now but also what we will require in the future. Our needs may change, but they will tend to change only slowly and in predictable ways. As a result of this permanence and predictability, housing is readily understandable to us. We know what constitutes good quality housing, and we need no experts to diagnose our requirements. There is an epistemic clarity to housing which opens it up to the ordinary sense of the world. The common rules by which it operates can be readily learned and accepted.

These epistemological qualities, linked to the ordinary sense of our world, cradle us and allow for our complacency to be maintained. We are readily able to absorb and assimilate elements from the external world. These external elements may change us, but we do not necessarily feel added to. We feel no distinct addition. We were already complete and remain so. We are in the midst of the world which we see as regular and a unity. We have incorporated the external into our sense of the ordinary. We are like a sponge: we do not expand but absorb, and so we keep to our natural limits.

Complacency is where we do not have to face the implacable. We cannot absorb the implacable. If we could, there would be no boundaries between us and the external world. Implacability in this sense is the opposite of complacency (King, 2017a). The implacable does not react, but it passively opposes.

However, complacency does mask the implacability of the dwelling. It turns implacability outwards so that it works on others rather than us. It opposes those outside dwelling. Implacability shields us and permits our complacency. As such, to be complacent means, or gives the appearance, that we have control and exclusive use of dwelling.

Complacency is to assume things can always be as they currently are. As such, it allows us to assimilate things from the outside without any apparent change in attitude and confidence. Complacency is the appearance of ambivalence to change based on a perception of the fixity of ourselves in a particular place. It is where we believe we can act on our own terms. Hence, the importance of absorption – the fact that we take things in – without apparent change. We assimilate and the new becomes like us, a part of us as we are. Something assimilated ceases to remain distinct. It is now an indistinguishable part of dwelling, part of what we take as ordinary.

But is it an illusion?

How much of dwelling is an illusion? It may be very comforting but is dwelling built on an illusion? Perhaps it might be seen as a necessary illusion. Dwelling can lull us with its consistency. The fact that it continues to work in a regular and consistent fashion means that we can forget our obligations and the complexity of what surrounds us.

The implacability of dwelling can help both maintain and break illusions. We can hide behind dwelling, but we can also find ourselves broken if we dash ourselves against it. Hiding in dwelling allows us to delude ourselves. We need not listen to anyone or see anyone, and we do not have to be told anything or say anything. The complacency of dwelling does not necessarily keep us honest. It can protect us from the truth and keep our illusions intact.

Dwelling itself is not an illusion: it most certainly exists. We need not be fooled or deluded by it. But it may have the ability to break down our illusions, as was the case when heating pumps break or when representatives of the landlord arrive to serve a Notice of Seeking Possession. So while it is easy to be deluded if we hide, unless we accept dwelling as it is, it will eventually let us down. If we do not maintain our relationship with dwelling, it will fail us, and the fault will be ours.

Illusion might be the reverse side of complacency. We are not prepared because we do not feel that we need to be: what can possibly go wrong for us? Dwelling is a place where it is not legitimate for us to be challenged. It is not proper, polite or civil. It would be an intrusion. In the workplace, we can be challenged if we do not fulfil our responsibilities, and this may happen quickly because we are letting others down. But in dwelling, this may not be the case: who, other than ourselves, are we letting down? We are not responsible to anyone but ourselves, and so we are not challenged. It is simply inappropriate to ask us to justify what we are doing.

Illusion can be maintained by the regularity of events within dwelling. Things continue on and we expect them to. Locking the door provides us with the illusion of security, and most of the time, our security is not threatened. Our precautions do work and so we can carry on. Of course, not all illusions are harmful, especially when we keep them to ourselves and they are literally kept within bounds. Dwelling means that we do not have to take our illusions anywhere or inflict them on anyone. Complacency gives us the authority to act just as we will. We are the rulers of our dwelling and we cannot be questioned. We are not being uncaring or selfish, but simply being completely at ease in something we know intimately. But this also allows us to forget issues and put them aside.

Appearances seem to matter

There is a tendency to separate the procurement of dwelling from its use. This tendency is obviously central to policy thinking, but we can also see it in the way that some individuals behave. We can use dwelling regardless of the ease or difficulty with which we are able to fund it. In my early days as a housing officer in the early 1980s, a colleague and I visited a household living in one of the housing association's properties. The house was a three-bedroom terraced house only a few years old on what was the most sought-after estate owned by the association. The tenants – a married couple with children – kept the dwelling immaculately. They were likewise well-dressed and well-spoken. The décor was tasteful to my inexperienced eye, and the furniture was new and clearly chosen to match a particular theme. All the appliances in the house seemed to be modern, including a particularly large television for the time. However, the reason for our visit – my colleague being the rent recovery officer – was that the couple had considerable rent arrears, amounting to several hundred pounds (this amounted to several months' rent at that time). Warning letters had been sent, which elicited no response, and so the purpose of our visit was to hand deliver the formal Notice of Seeking Possession documents.

It became immediately clear that the husband was completely unaware of the rent arrears, believing that his wife was taking care of the payments. I am sure that this led to some considerable difficulties in the marriage, but as the debt was quite quickly cleared, I have no more knowledge of what occurred. However, the issue for me then, and whenever I have thought about it since, was the disparity between the manner in which they had made and maintained their dwelling, at some considerable expense and with no little effort, and their failure to pay their legally due rent to their landlord. This was not the only time I came across a case such as this, where an apparently comfortable household was in rent arrears, but I was, and still am, confused as to why someone would do this. The tenants appeared competent and had been with the association for several years. They were not unintelligent and could not be unaware of their legal obligations to their landlord. They were both in full-time employment and seemed to take good care of their children.

Of course, I am dealing here with appearances, and it may have been that there were further financial difficulties which the wife had kept from her husband. There might have been other debts alongside the rent arrears. The wife was perhaps then prioritising what needed to be paid most urgently and considered the landlord to be more flexible than other agencies (which was probably true at that time). She may well have hoped to sort out her financial troubles without her husband having to know about them. However, a small debt had turned into a large one and she had found it hard to clear it and, once the deception had begun, it became impossible to stop. The consequences of admitting the deception became more severe the longer it was maintained. Each day that she did not hear from the landlord (or because they only sent warning letters that she could hide or destroy) seemed to validate her decision to keep the debt from her husband. She could believe that she would get away with it. But inevitably, the problem was only getting worse and there came a point when it could no longer be avoided.

At issue, here is the separation between regarding the dwelling as a place of comfort, refuge and status, and the prioritising the need to pay for it. In my experience, it was much more common for households who did not pay their rent also to neglect their dwelling: they had no money for rent, appliances or decoration. But here was a household who clearly had sufficient resources to fund a decent lifestyle and maintain their property to a standard well above what was typical for the association's tenants. They had a tastefully appointed dwelling, due to their own efforts and their own expense, but they had neglected their rent payments. Was it just that not paying the rent was easier and apparently less consequential than paying for groceries or credit card bills? Was this the wife's particular responsibility, with her husband funding the rest? But whatever the reason, there was a clear distinction at work here between the use of dwelling and its financing. These two aspects can and do operate independently of each other, even though neither can be ignored indefinitely. Housing costs will vary, more than use tends to. We do not tend to cut down on use proportionately when costs increase, and the reason for this is that, quite simply, we cannot. We can either use the dwelling or we cannot: it is all or nothing. We may cut down on the usage of certain utilities in the dwelling and that may circumscribe our use to an extent. But our general use of dwelling, as a place of exclusion and care, continues until it stops completely because we are forced to leave. But up to that point, we retain complete control over the dwelling, and we have total use of it. Our control over the dwelling does not alter as the financial situation changes.

We use the dwelling as if we have paid for it outright, even though for most households the costs are ongoing and are, to an extent, variable. While we may take out loans for other items, the repayments are never as prolonged as mortgage repayments over decades, or rent payment for ever. Also, the consequence of defaulting on other loans is less consequential: having our car repossessed may cause us considerable difficulties and affect our livelihood, but it does not generally carry the same existential threat as homelessness.

Why is paying for dwelling not always the highest priority? Why, for some at least, is there a distinction between dwelling and asset? I think that at least part of the answer lies in the taken-for-granted nature of dwelling. The functions of dwelling are so embedded into our routines and practices. Dwelling is regular and apparently unchanging, and it supports all our other activities. The use of dwelling involves no particular effort. Being habitual, it appears to lack consequentiality: it is never out of the ordinary. There is no credit or debit to it, unlike a bank account where any changes are transparent and the effects obviously consequential. Dwelling helps us hide from the consequentiality and inevitability of our actions.

What we are attached to

I am very attached to my particular dwelling and I would say I have an affection for it. It holds so many memories for me. I have lived there all my married life, and my wife and I raised our two children there. I wrote all of my books there. We have gone through an awful lot in that place. But I seldom look at it, or even consider it. I do not look at it, for example, in the way I notice my wife, as someone who is so special to me and whom it is impossible to take for granted (and who would never let me do so).

I do not consider my dwelling in the same way that I would think about a book I have enjoyed and savoured. I do not linger over my dwelling. I just expect it to be there. Even when I am writing about it, as I am now, I have my head down and I am focusing on getting my thoughts down in my notebook. I am not looking at my dwelling as I write about it. I am in it and it holds me, but I am focusing on something else.

This, though, is precisely how dwelling works. We do not have to look at something we know will always be there. Indeed, it is entirely because I am comfortable and at ease here that I can ignore it. I do not need to notice something which does what it is meant to do without show or complaint. My affection for my dwelling lies in its very passivity, and as such, it is a very different form of affection from that which I have towards my wife and daughters.

There are many things in my dwelling that I do not notice. I glide through it without really seeing it. I do this because it remains as I expect it to be. I would only notice things if they were different from how they ought to be. Accordingly, when we do look properly, we can be surprised by what we see. Here is something distinct and palpable, something hard and unyielding.

But it is also something that is worn, that shows signs of our presence. It carries our marks and we start to remember things. Our eyes drift to pictures and ornaments, objects that carry a particular feeling with them. We recall memories related to these singular things, and soon we are lost again. And we have stopped looking *at* the dwelling. We are now thoroughly absorbed *in* dwelling. We are immersed in it as the meanings attached to things bloom in front of us. They are no longer just memories, and the dwelling is no longer a hard and unyielding object. We have moved into that particular enclosed space that only dwelling can make. We are carried away into some other realm of daydreams and reveries that Gaston Bachelard (1969) described so acutely. We are now in a place where all we are and all we have just is.

To take someone or something for granted is not to revere them or hold them in great affection. It would appear we are being offhand and disrespectful if we treat a person in this way. Treating an object in a similar manner might also be to misuse it and show disrespect. But not with dwelling. We really do have to take it for granted. We cannot use it while looking adoringly at it. We cannot note how important and special it is in our lives *and* carry on with those lives. We have to ignore it and treat it in an offhand way as if it will always be there when we require it and without complaint. The greatest compliment we can pay dwelling is to take it for granted. It is a tool and is best not seen as distinct from the tasks we have for it.

So to ask if I have affection for my dwelling is actually a rather odd question. I feel I ought to say 'yes'. I am deeply attached to it and I intend to stay in it. But this is because it has proved particularly effective as the background to my life, and I have been able to ignore it and use it as I please. My attachment, therefore, needs to remain implicit and unconscious.

In some ways, I feel that I do not even know my dwelling very well, in that I drift through it without giving it any real attention. I can walk from room to room in the dark. I know what to expect, where things are. But as I do this, I do not scrutinise what I am doing. I would only have to think if things were not where I expected them to be.

My dwelling is a container, a box, and I can look at it as such. I can see it as a physical object. But I seldom do. I am almost always doing something within it that depends on the box but is not because of the box, it is not *for* the box or *with* the box. The box is incidental to the activity, even as I know that I could not do it outside the box.

The significance of dwelling is that it retains the appearance of being incidental while holding me and mine safely and securely. It is then, in truth, the very opposite of incidental, but it can only remain so by never letting its significance become apparent.

Dwelling is made invisible, it is transparent to consciousness, by our use of it. We lose sight of it as a thing in itself. We do not see its complexity, cost or consequentiality. Indeed, we might go so far as to say that dwelling needs us to forget about it in order to work as it should. It needs to become a tool. So, I can properly say that I seldom look at my dwelling. Of course, I have my eyes open when I walk up to it and open the door. I have to know where to put the key. Likewise, I tend to have my eyes open when descending the stairs. By not looking, I mean I do not see my dwelling as a distinct entity. I do not often inspect it or look it over for defects or signs of wear. I trust that it will remain as it is. I do not look at the state of the brickwork or the roof tiles. I do not notice small changes in décor, or even whether it needs a good clean or not. If things get beyond a certain point, or if we have been away for a while, then we might look around and notice things we need to attend to. But day to day, I simply do not notice. I know more about the external fabric of my neighbours' dwellings than my own. I see them every time I look out of my window, but I cannot see my own.

There are some parts of our dwelling where we linger, and others where we do not. Over the last 30 years, I have spent countless hours staring at my bedroom ceiling, trying to sleep or not wanting to get up. I know certain shapes and patterns in the artex that have almost become friends. These are in the shapes of animals (dogs and sharks seem to feature prominently), human or near-human heads and figures and other interesting shapes, all pieced together out of my imagination. As well, there are familiar noises in the dwelling, such as the crack of the roof joists as they cool in the evening, the sound of the heating system (which usually does work) and the slightly muffled sound of the radio from the kitchen or the living room. These are comforting sounds of normality and bring with them a sense of recognition. But there are other spaces where I spend much less time, particularly those spaces we use predominantly for storage such as the loft and the garage.

We use different parts of the dwelling in different ways. The kitchen and the study are both work in the two places spaces although the nature of the work is different with little similarity between them. The kitchen is for household maintenance – cooking, cleaning – while the study is for intellectual work. Kitchen work is more obviously and directly productive – meals, clean clothes – but the study is where I did the work that I was paid to do and that provided the resources to buy food and clothing.

There are some who maintain a strict demarcation between and, indeed, within spaces. I will often work on the bed, either first thing in the morning or for an hour or so or during the day. While she tolerates this behaviour, my wife does not approve of it in the least and would seldom do the same. She has often told me of the importance of separating work and leisure and keeping these spaces distinct. But I am happy to write anywhere – in my study, bedroom, living rooms, pubs and cafés, trains and buses. I can do this as the need arises. However, when my family are in the house, I will use the study so that I can concentrate and not impose on the others. My wife and daughters will sit in the garden as often as they can, depending on the weather. I will seldom do this, preferring to work with music on and with my laptop and phone to hand. My wife needs silence to work, but I prefer to have music on.

I know of some academics who refuse to work at home. They will not even check their work emails once they have left their office. One or two scholars I have known will only write in their offices and only between 9 and 5, Monday to Friday. However, nearly all my research, writing and teaching preparation has been done at home, and not necessarily within normal working hours. I wrote my first two books largely in the evenings and over weekends, but this was when I had a heavy teaching load, and young children who went to bed early. As time went by, I could work from home more often and took advantage of this. I still work at all hours, some-times until midnight and over weekends. Having said that, I will happily take two hours off during the day to go for lunch with my wife.

So, I do not distinguish in any major way between work and home, or in the places where I am prepared to work. This means that I use dwelling in a particular manner that might be more unstructured or flexible than some others. I do not necessarily recommend it as a model, and it does depend on a number of factors. I had a very flexible employer who allowed me consid-erable latitude. I had to be in a classroom as per timetable and at meetings as required, but other than that, I could work where I wished. Technology allowed me to stay in touch with work. I could access the university network and email system remotely. Broadband and the advent of the laptop have allowed me to work anywhere in the house. For much of the day, I had the house to myself. My homeworking coincided with my children reaching school age, and so, I was free to work for a large part of the day. But my work patterns have also had a lot to do with my attitude towards dwelling. I prefer to be at home and feel most comfortable here. Moreover, my work was decidedly lo-tech (laptop, pen, notebook, books) and I need no special facilities to undertake my research. Beyond this, I greatly depend on the tolerance of the people I live with. We are prepared to accommodate each other and have established the requisite routines. We have always had the physical space to allow us to do what we want in different parts of the house without disturbing each other.

Now we might ask whether this discussion on the use of dwelling means anything significant? Perhaps it does not, other than the fact that the dwell-ing is flexible and can accommodate different modes of living in the same space. This is, to an extent, dependent on the amount of space we have, the level of technology we can access and who, if anyone, we share the space with. All I can say is that given the choice, I would doubtless always have preferred to work from home and found a career path that allowed me to do this, aided by technology and a loving relationship. Of course, I live in first world conditions, but these conditions allow me to live and work in the same place just as my pre-capitalist ancestors would have done.[7]

Perhaps the real relevance of this discussion is that the very manner in which I use dwelling has influenced the way I write about it. Where I work has impacted on the work itself and directly in terms of subject matter. I write about dwelling from within it, and I think that this situation matters. I have a particular stance on dwelling conditioned by my own use of dwelling. The study of the subjective here depends quite properly on the subjectivity of the circumstances of its composition. As such, the boundary that is dwelling is not merely or even primarily defensive. The boundary is not there merely to protect us. It also exists to help define us, to show us what we are. A boundary condenses meaning. It holds us in place, allowing us to associate meaning with a tightly defined space.

7 As stated in the preface, this essay was written before the lockdowns of 2020 and 2021. This has altered the way in which many people have had to use their dwelling and how they have worked: my daughter, for example, had to work at home for most of the period between March 2020 and July 2021 and continues to do so for two days per week. However, my own patterns of working and living before 2020 proved to be rather effective training for lockdown and I have had to change my habits very little.

References

Bachelard, G (1969): *The Poetics of Space*, Boston, Beacon.
Dreyfus, H (2014): *Skillful Coping: Essays on the Phenomenology of Everyday Perception and Action*, edited by Mark Wrathall, Oxford, Oxford University Press.
Freud, S (2003): *The Uncanny*, London, Penguin.
Fromm, E (1995): *The Art of Loving*, London, Thorsons.
Gould, T (2003): 'The Names of Action', in Eldridge, R (Ed.): *Stanley Cavell*, Cambridge, Cambridge University Press, pp. 48–78.
Heidegger, M (1962): *Being and Time*, Oxford, Blackwell.
Heidegger, M (1971): 'Building, Dwelling, Thinking', in *Poetry, Language, Thought*, New York, Harper and Row, pp. 145–61.
King, P (1996): *The Limits of Housing Policy: A Philosophical Investigation*, London, Middlesex University Press.
King, P (2003): *A Social Philosophy of Housing*, Aldershot, Ashgate.
King, P (2004): *Private Dwelling: Contemplating the Use of Housing*, London, Routledge.
King, P. (2005): *The Common Place: The Ordinary Experience of Housing*, Aldershot, Ashgate.
King, P. (2008): *In Dwelling: Implacability, Exclusion and Acceptance*, Aldershot, Ashgate.
King, P (2014): *The Antimodern Condition: An Argument Against Progress*, Farnham, Ashgate.
King, P (2017a): *Thinking on Housing: Words, Memories, Use*, Abingdon, Routledge.
King, P (2017b): *Living Alone, Living Together: Two Essays on the Use of Housing*, Bingley, Emerald.
Le Corbusier (1927): *Towards a New Architecture*, London, Butterworth.
Le Corbusier (1929): *The City of Tomorrow*, London, Butterworth.
Ligotti, T (2015): *Songs of a Dead Dreamer and Grimscribe*, London, Penguin Classics.
Ligotti, T (2018): *The Conspiracy against the Human Race: A Contrivance of Horror*, London, Penguin.
Morley, D (2000): *Home Territories: Media, Mobility and Identity*, London, Routledge.

Norberg-Schulz, C (1985): *The Concept of Dwelling: On the Way to a Figurative Architecture*, New York, Rizzoli.

Oliver, P (2003): *Dwellings: The Vernacular House Worldwide*, London, Phaidon.

Peterson, J (2018): *12 Rules for Life: An Antidote to Chaos*, London, Allen Lane.

Rosen, S (2002): *The Elusiveness of the Ordinary: Studies in the Possibility of Philosophy*, New Haven, Yale University Press.

Schopenhauer, A (1969): *The World as Will and Representation*, two volumes, London, Dover.

Turner, J. (1976): *Housing by People: Towards Autonomy in Building Environments*, London, Marion Boyars.

Index

For Product Safety Concerns and Information please contact our EU
representative GPSR@taylorandfrancis.com
Taylor & Francis Verlag GmbH, Kaufingerstraße 24, 80331 München, Germany

www.ingramcontent.com/pod-product-compliance
Lightning Source LLC
Chambersburg PA
CBHW061839220326
41599CB00027B/5337

* 9 7 8 1 0 3 2 2 5 2 7 7 3 *